YSMAEL'S POEMS

PART II

My Ancestors

YET II

Ysmael Tisnado II

Ysmael's Poems Part II
Copyright © 2025 by Ysmael Tisnado II

ISBN: 979-8894791814 (sc)

ISBN: 979-8894791821 (e)

The Reading Glass
BOOKS

The Reading Glass Books
1-888-420-3050
www.readingglassbooks.com
production@readingglassbooks.com

Allora = Then

Allora Io andò a la via per la mia casa.= Then I go to the street by
my house. Aspetto i miei amici a chi andiamo. = I wait and with
my friends I go. Io sono felice perché il giorno comincia bene
per me.= I am Happy because the day started well for me.

Tutto assicurati che qualcuna volta troppo veloce = Everything
is secured that one time very fast. Nessuno conosce la ragione
per essere. = No one knows the reason. Siamo pacifico per
la strada sulla città. = We are peaceful on the street with the
city. Dunque una cosa dolce per Io. = So it's a sweet thing for
me. Vorace per la pace in DIO. = Voracious for the peace in
GOD. Solo un giorno aspettiamo di te salvatore. = Only a day
waiting for you Saviour. Dietro una sinagoga il mashiach viene
per noi. = Inside the synagogue the Messiah comes for us.

02/07/23

Antorcha=Torch

Se derrocha la antorcha al vino se le quita la corcha = It wastes
the torch to wine they take of the cork. Yo pinto con una brocha la
comida se sancocha.= I paint with a brush and the food is parboiled.
Los Peruanos adoran a Viracocha con la coca es muy poca. = The
Peruvians adore Viracocha with Coca leaves is it very little. = El
cacao es el manjar de un lao en asopao.= The cacao is the delicacy
of one side in the soup. Un tigre está dentro de una piragua que
va de Nicaragua a ala capital Managua. = A tiger was inside the
pirogue that goes to Nicaragua to the capital Managua. Aguas
frescas que chupa la cabra.= Fruit flavored waters that the goat eats.
Es para mi tío que abra.= Is for my uncle to open. Soy un corazón
que no pierde la razón. = I am heart that doesn't lose the reason.
Me maravillo de las pirámides que son verdades sin falsedades.=I
marvel at the pyramids that are truths without falsehoods.

03/21/23

1

April Fool's

April Fool's have lost the rules. I seem to Joke now you're broke. In April I eat meat staple. I stick around the town with a whining hound. Let's see the breeze for a tease. To a condo beachfront lease who am I to appease. Oh jeez please. I know I can still dig with a hoe. Everyone is behind for a quick fixed solution. Drinking Hibiscus for an infusion. I go to the beach to teach how to swim on a whim. No one's thinking it's me breaking doing the nickel makes me fickle for a tickle. We dance for money trickle for my honey.

04/01/23

Abstract East

From Eretzs Yisrael to Hindustan to Nippon from Middle East to Indian Subcontinent to far East. I look for prosperity to the feast. It's all not the least. I see Magen David, Hindu glyph to Yen. I sense these Oriental men that I look at with an interesting lens. Money or culture to comprehend all the Orient will lend its expertise in treating disease. Is it ignorance or knowledge that will cease? It's our longing. It's our longing to appease and please. The abstract East to Middle East. So the plethoras will have many amphoras.

04/18/23

Ahora Si = Now Yes

Ahora si: Gloria a Dios = Glory be to God.

Alzo mi voz: = I raise my voice. Junto los dos : = Together us two.

Ahora si: Voy por el sendero de luz no soy avestruz.
= I go by the trail of light I am not an ostrich.

Ahora si: Ahora si: Ahora si: Ahora si:

Gracias Padre santo por mi pan celestial.= I thank you heavenly father.

El Paraiso es un manantial.= The Paradise is a running spring.

Jesus mi se~nor tu eres esa flor junto con el espiritu santo porque yo
canto.= Jesus my lord you are the flower with the holy spirit why I sing.

Andamos hacia al cielo con los angeles pero no cibeles. We are
going towards the sky with the angels but not the cybels.

Ahora si : Un suspiro de cual yo miro sin retiro.= A sigh of which
I see without retirement. Gracias mi Dios.= Thanks my God.

Ahora no Ahora si esto me dices asi.= Now no
now yes this you te l me like this.

09/08/20

A Borboleta= The Butterfly

A borboleta nao pode comprar o ar so voar pelas nuvens.= The butterfly cannot buy the air only fly through the clouds.

Ele cocoonse numa mortalha= It cocoons itself in a shroud.

Quando a larva transformase.= When a larva transforms itself.

Ele longo ser liberta voar por ceu.= It longs
to be free to fly through the sky.

E faixa de asas as flores por todo as horas.= Its wings
span the flowers throughout the hours.

Regular para polenque pule.= Even for pollen it scours.

Para seu alimento transforma em nectar.=For
its food it transforms into nectar.

E cores sao um infindavel de espectro.= It's
colors are a myriad of specter.

O amarelo e e tom principal.= Yellow is its main hue.

Ao adeus de borboleta.= To the butterfly adieu.

Com manchas pretas em seu envergadura.=With
black spots in its wingspan.]

Ligue os pontos se pode.=Connect the dots if you can.

11/27/09

Ahora Una Flora = Now The Flora

Papa a ti te enviamos una rosa a tu tumba en camino a mi tia concha. = Dad to you we send a rose to your tomb on the way to Aunt Concha.

Espero que te guste esta rosa que viene de mi y tu esposa.= I hope you like the rose that comes from me and your wife.

No se cuando te soñaré solo Dios lo sabe todo aún tenemos que pedirle permiso para todo.= I don't know when I will dream you only G-D know everything even though that we want to ask him permission for everything.

Bueno pa esta flor es para ti.=Well dad the flower is for you.

Aquí vamos en camino.= Here we come on the way.

02/16/20

Ahora Que?= Now What?

Ahora que hacemos? = Now what do we do?

No se puede salir.= We can not go outside.

Estamos confinados a nuestros hogares.=
We are confined to our hearths.

Como el mio Cid los cantares.= Like the Mio Cid the songs.

?Cuando vamos a respirar una solucion a nuestro problema?=When
are we going to breathe a solution to our problems?

!Hasta cuando DIOS mio podremos salir al encuentro comunitario
si yo me llamo Dario!= !When will we G-D be able to come out
to our community encounter if I am not named Darius!

Leer,ver pensar es el ejercicio sin Dionisio.=Read,
see , think is the exercise without Dionises.

Dios mediante en suplicio hay que rendir servicio.=
G-D be willing to suplice now render service.

?Cuando vamos a sentir aliento de un viento?=When
are we going to feel a breath of fresh air?

Aqui ahora bella se~nora.= Here and now beautiful lady.

Quiero vivir otra vez.= I want to live again.

Una solucion para todo el mundo.= A solution for all the world.

!Ahora que distancia social comer tortillas con queso
en el temascal!= !Now what distance social to eat
tortillas with cheese in the sweat lodge.

Dios queremos otra oportunidad no castigo con impunidad.= G-D
we want another opportunity to no punishment with impunity.

Sereno quiero ser que venga el sol para vencer.=
Serene I want to be the sun that defeats.

Otro dia de salud sin una vicitud.= Another day of health without a vice.
?Ahora Que?=?Now What?

4/12/20

Ancora Che Fai=Still What We Do

Ancora come io Faccio la mia vita?=Still how do I do my life?

Una domanda ce Qual Cuna?= One question is it someone?

Sempre per me ieri come io fato?= Always for
me yesterday how I have done?

Solo Dio sapeva la ragione perche.= Only God knows the reason why.

Mai sapevo come andare per incontrare la soluzione a miei
problemi.=I never know how I go to fin the solution to my problems.

Io so la verita di la mia situazione financiale.= I
know the truth of my financia situation.

Ci sono un altra verita che fai ancora.=They
are one other truth that do now.

La situazione e per pagare debti il soldi chi pagano allora.=The
situation is to pay debts the money that pays now.

Soltanto Io ho il tempo che Dio me dai per questo Io sai.=
Only i have the time that G-D gives me for this I know.

Io dico grazzi a Dio per darmi tempo per soluzionare
miei predicamenti.= I say thanks to G-D for giving
me time to resolve my predicaments.

Aspetto come rincominciare la vita di nouvo.=
I wait to restart life a new.

Sei per me Dio chi me aiutare e come me supera.=
It's for me G-D who helped is how I survive.

Per il momento IO vuoi la pace internale per andare fronte la
vita.=For the moment I want the internal peace to go on with life.

Solo io sai la riposta a mia vita non solo gli soldi.=Only
I know the reply to my life not only money.

04/22/20

Adonay Pasensya=GOD Patience

Adonay do mi pasensya para no konduizir.=GOD
give me patience to not drive,

Esto merrekiado ken non puedo andar en oto.=I
am sad that I can't be in an auto.

No me deshes en mi angustya porke no puedo konduzir en el oto.=
Don't leave me in my agony because I can't drive in a automobile.

Hashem dami la konfiensa ke yo vo poder andar
konduziendo en dos anyos.=GOD give me the confidence
that I will be able to drive in two years.

Ayudami sinyor para ke kadal diya mijori mi tyempo i aspera bueno.=
Help me lord for each day I improve in my time and wait well.

Dom la salu sin desmayos agora i syempre. = Give
me health without siezures now and forever.

Ke kada sesh meses se kumpla todo byen i ke el neurologo
me di el visto bueno.=That each six months finishes all
well and that the neurologist gives me his blessing.

Yo kero voltar andar en mi araba konduziendo presto mijor ke nunkua.=
I want to return to drive in my car driving fast better than ever.

Aspero en ti mi DYOke oigas mis tefilot ke mis dezeyos
seyan para bueno.= I wait in you my GOD that you hear
my prayers that my desires will be for good.

Ayudami presto i ke se ponga fin a mi problema de konduizir.=
Help me fast and put an end to my problem of driving.

Ten veluntad buena kon mi i abolti en oto.= Have
good will with me and return me to the car.

08/05/20

Ahora Que Espera= Now What Awaits

Ahora que espera el dia mera mera.=Now
what awaits the day verily I say.

DIOS mediante tengo techo sin despecho.= GOD be
willing I have a roof over me without spite.

Duermo en un lecho de provecho.= I sleep in a bed of providence.

Hecho tiempo adelante viviendo cada instante todo adelante.=
I have made time ahead living each instant all ahead.

Yo suspiro por una morada y todo que sea dada.= I
sigh for an abode and everything that is given.

Me encomiendo a DIOS para que escuche mi voz.= I put
myself in God's hands for him to hear my voice.

Solo no en dos mi situación tiene emoción.= Only
not in two my situation has emotion.

El tiempo corre avante todo DIOS mediante.=
Time goes before all God 's willing.

Estando yo en la víspera del tiempo todo lo siento.=
I begin on the eve of time all I feel.

No hay duda en mi pensamiento.= There is no doubt in my thinking.

Ahora voy el día estipulado como si fuera apostolado.= Now
I go to the day stipulated like if it were apostolate.

Solo DIOS tiene razón tocando mi corazón.= Only
GOD has the reason touching my heart.

Ahora que espera en la diáspora sin tocar la tambora.= Now
what awaits in the diaspora without playing the drum.

Hay solución que viene de DIOS para todo tiene su apodo.= There
is a solution that comes from GOD for all who have his nickname.

Ahora que espera sin la carraspera.=Now what awaits a ticks rasp.

08/31/20

Agora Vou Manter Ocupado=Now I Have To Maintain

Muitas vezes eu procuro estar ocupado com a música.
=Many times I look to be busy with music.

Ninguém saiba porque eu sinto assim pra que todo
o som é pra lá.=No one knows why I feel like this for
everything the sound and for over there.

Tudo isso foi muito bom pra mim.=All that was very good for me.

Nesta música vou manter ocupada a minha jornada
pra trabalhar ainda mais.= This music I will maintain
busy to my journey to work even more.

Ocupado me satisfaz sempre andando a rasta do pé porque eu tenho a
fé.= Busy I am satisfied always dragging my foot because I have faith.

Isto é muito difícil para estar ocupado sempre cada dia.=It
is very difficult to always be occupied each day.

O sol sai no verão e deixa estar quente do calor.=The sun
comes out the summer and leaves in the warmth.

Pra mim sozinho no mais com minha mãe isso é difícil não
estar com minhas amizades.= For me alone it is more with
my mother that is and difficult not to be with my friends.

Terça feira ir a igreja com meu irmão Justin com toda a congregação
em Santee um dia da semana.= Tuesday go to the church with my
brother Justin with all the congregation in Santee one day of the week.

Por conviver com todo mundo por isso eu quero ir a
igreja manter ocupado.= To break bread with everyone.
For that I want to go to church to keep busy.

Isto é para mim muito bom, me dá sonoridade de viver felizmente.=
This is for me very good, it gives me the sound to live happily.

09/02/20

Anyada Buena Alegre=Happy New Year

Anyada buena alegre.

Yo kero dizir para bendizir.= I want to say to bless.

La felisida inchir mi korason.=The happiness will fill my heart.

Sin bivir en teror la pas les do de dor en dor.= Without living
in terror the peace I give to generation to generation.

Ke no mankemos pas i djustisiya lus sentimyentos avlan al interyor.=
That we never lack peace and justice the feelings speak to the interior.

De muestro DIO ansi a mi me plase muncho.= Of
our GOD even though it pleases me much.

Ainde no es leshana tova ma anyo sekularo.=Still it is not the
Religious Happy New Year but the secular New Year.

Tengamos kaminos de leche i myel ke mos proteja el andjel.=That
we have roads of milk and honey that the angel will protect us.

Pujados i no amenguados la reushita yena.=
Multiplied and not diminished a full success.

I buena una anyada mazalada.= And good a lucky year.

All The Way

Hey all the way.

I am going to lay come what may.

I may not stay for the clothes on lay-away.

Things are not cheap nor do they lie on a heap.

They are expensive which makes me pensive.

Should I could I yes or no.

I can't go with the flow.

Spending money like it were honey during the holidays.

Chanuka, Christmas, Kwanza and Eid Al Fitir.

So many feasts seem queer.

Many a time I drop a tear.

Crying about how expensive the cost.

Emptying my money lost.

All the way in a daze gone on a shopping craze.

I got the blues from my neck up down to my shoes.

I am glad I not drinking booze.

I can't do credit I will need a medic.

Ande Vo Agora= Where I Am Going Now.

Ande vo agora no tengo sinyora.= Where I
am going now I don't have a lady.

Munchos mi dizin ke vo fazer yo un eksmiliter.= Many
have said to me what is a exmilitary going to do.

En mi mueva sivadad no efasar la mueva kapasidad.=
In my new city not to erase the new capacity.

No ambezo ande sto ainde yo me vo.= I don't
learn where I am even though I go.

Todo lo vo ambezar endeagora komo una meldadora.=
Everything I am going to lear from now on like a reader.

Yo tengo ke endevinar para aboltar.=I must divine to return.

El kamino aki en Temecula es la mueva mabula.= The
road here in Temecula is the new deluge.

Porke mi lealta es San Diego.= For my loyal is San Diego.

No se si puedo trokar muncho tyempo stava en sivdad grande.=
I don't know if I can change much time I was in the big city.

No me muero de ambre.= I don't die of hunger.

Agora bivo en un gran kazal.= Now I live in
a great place outside of Istanbul.

Ke para mi no es mazal.= Which is not good luck.

Adios Temecula= Goodbye Temecula

Jamas volvere a Temecula.=I'm never coming back to Temecula.

Hola mi San Diego querido por Temecula me despido.=
Hi San Diego dear for Temecula I say farewell.

Vuelvo a ti san Diego mi nido.= I return to you San Diego my nest.

Ahora soy feliz como la raiz.=Now I am happy like a root.

A la chingada con mi mana.= To hell with my sissy.

A la verga con mi cu~nao.= Fuck my in laws.

Mira en que hado yo estado.= Look in what destiny I have been.

No mas abuso financiero por fin llega mi recreo fiestero.= No
more financial abuse at last comes my festive recess.

Borron y cuenta nueva ya me sali de la cueva.=
Fresh new slate I got out of my cave.

Agora Abolto = Now I Return

Abolta la ojika por mi kerida sivdadika.= Turn
the page for my dear little city.

Kon mi puerpo di repente me desha kontente.= With
my body all of a sudden it leaves me happy.

Kumida Sefaradiya unas buenas rechetas.=Sephardic
food some good recipes.

Birmuelos i kave turko agora abclto.= Sweet
patties and Turkish coffee now I return.

Ande sta mi rengrasyo al Dio?= Where is my thanks to GOD?

So muy ahava olam chesed ve rachamim.= I am very
loving world acts of kindness and mercy.

Yo kero ir a mi tyerra natala!= I want to go to my native land!

Munchos mushos al kadar komemos i bebemos a eskapar.=
Many lips to up to we eat and drink to get out.

Alive

I am alive in San Diego.

No longer will try to we go.

I am back in my neck of the woods.

For me trading goods back out of Temecula.

Rent or buy somewhere.

As long as I care.

I will not dare.

I am reborn like the roses with their thorns.

No more locking horns.

I am free to be me.

Free as the eye can see.

A Young Man

A young man from another planet.

A young man said who am I.

Im in a camp surrounded by strange beings.

Mean, despicable, violent get me out of here.

How will I be free of them?

Against the odds of their huge size, technology advanced.

I must come up with a plan.

I need people who will rise up.

Let my people go said Moses to Phaoroah
the Israeite like odyssey begins.

Based on a story by Jeremy Tiefenbrun.

Ande Esto = Where Am I

En ke hal me an metido?!=In what situation have they put me!

Ya no tengo a mis chaverim!=I don't have my friends!

Ainde yo so uno de los anousim.=Even though
I am one of the forcibly converted.

E pedrido la musa de mis flores.= I have lost the muse of my flowers.

Ande yo estuvi enflorado.= Where I flourished.

Los poemas se an amenguado.= The poems have been diminished.

Por falta de inspirasyon.= For lack of inspiration.

Ansi es mi emosion.= So is my emotion.

Kero aboltar a San Diego.= I want to return to San Diego.

Ayi es mi kontente.= There I am content.

Todo lo deshi mientres.= Everything I left it meanwhile.

Esto soliko sin amista.= I am alone without friends.

Mas aleshado de la komunita.= More away from the community.

Ande esto a San Diego me vo.= Where I am to San Diego I go.

En dos anyos abolto.= In two years I return.

Para atras ma a trokado.= For going back but it has changed.

Another Day

Another day I spend trying to mend.

To learn my languages and drivers ed as I sit in bed.

I am over rested this day is not detested.

I watered the grass its soemthing I pass.

Monday is time to take out the trash.

I went to the bank to deposit the cash.

I had no bash I hid the stash.

Another day I did something.

Picked up the mail no thanks to no avail.

Or go to the library its in Temecula not Mayberry.

Bichiami = *What Are You Called*

Come ti chiami ?= What is your name? Bichiami Ysmael Bengiamino.= I am called Ysmael Benjamin. Sono celibato senza una donna.= I'm single without a woman. Un uomo che richiama amore. = I'm a man that requires love. Dove la mia fiore? = Where is my flower? Abbastanza e la balanza un giorno ritorno a te.= Abundance and balance a day I return to you. Solo io anda la.= Only I go yonder. Soltanto io sono una anima.= Only I am a soul. Si vai come fai amica.= If you come make a friend. Allora andiamo le due al mercato.= Still we are going to the market. Anche non sono sabato.= Even though it's not saturday. Mangiamo un piatto di spaghetti. We eat a plate of spaghetti. Dove canta una canzone di Santa Madre e Padre dal cuore.= Where we sing a song to the Holy Mother and Father of the heart.

02/10/23

Borekas = *Turnovers Snack*

Borekitas kon chay i leche en asukar de bevyenda. = Little turnovers with tea and milk with sugar as beverage. Es una deliziosa merienda al DIO Santo Bendicho yo rengrasyo. = It is a delicious snack to GOD Holy Blessed I thank. Agora aspero la more de klasa de komida. = Now I wait for the teacher of the nutrition class. Un a modrida y komo el reyenado adyentro las borekas kon su gomo.= A bite and a stuffing inside the turnovers with their fillings. Munchas vesez mi nona mos amostra lo salado de las borkitas ke los turkos yaman borek. = Many times my grandma showed us the saltiness of the little turnovers that the Turks call borek. Yo so sefardi se ke las borekas tyenen keso i espinakas o kartof i keso para Alhat.= I am Sephardic I know that the borkekas have cheese and spinach or potato and cheese. Rechetas kero di mi aguela ay muncho ke ambezar i fazer. = Recipes that I want from my grandmother to learn and do.

03/13/23

Bella = Beauty

Una donna bella richiama tempo ed amore in una relazione.= A beautiful woman reclaims time and love in a relationship. Non sono Sylvester Stallone.=Im not Sylvester Stallone. Io non sono bianco e nero ma marrone. = I'm not white or black but tan. Dove stai la vita dolce ce qualcuna. = Where is the sweet life that is some. Come Io mangiare una tuna.= Like I eat a tuna. Quella prima volta siamo amici dopo innamorati.= That first time we were friends and later lovers. Perche Io namoro della bellezza di donna sui capelli biondi e gli occhiali azzurri. = Because I fell in love with the beauty of the woman with her blond hair and blue eyes. Per me enamoro di quella.= For me I fell in love with that. Io fortunato la forza della vita.= I am fortunate in the force of life. La signorina mi dici bichiami Io sono Ysmael = The miss says to me what are you called? I am Ysmael.

03/16/23

Beausoleil = Beautiful Sun

IL fait beau aujourdhuis.= It's a good day today. Je me sens mieux que l' autre jour.= I feel better than the other day. Depuis je fait beaucoup de chansons pour chanter a le so eil de Californie Sud.= Later I made many songs to sing to the sun of Southern California. C'est la vie que regarder pour moi est bien merci a Dieu. = It is the life that sees that I look for me. It is good thanks to G-D. Toutes les choses ameliore en plus pour nos amis. =All the things improve in addition for our friends. J'ai la confiance de faire la bonne' a les gens de mon état. = I have the confidence to do good to people of my state. Nous réchauffer pour le froid. = We would warm up for the cold. J'attend L'occasion de ma patrie. = I'm waiting for the occasion of my country. Aux Etats-Unis c'est gagner de l'argent internationalement.= The United States that wins the money internationally. J'ai regardé ma mère au Mexique.= I have a look for my mom in Mexico. Nous regardons il mystique.= We look at the mystic.

03/24/23

Betrayal

Betrayal by Drew Westfield and Nicolette.

How could you Drew!

I thought we were friends.

Two or three years ago you did not act this way.

Why could you not tell me the truth?

Don't call me!

Don't bother me!

Don't visit me anymore!

You had to use your girlfriend as your mouthpiece to say no!

To say so!

There you go.

Drew, how could you!

If I knew, I thought we were friends.

But you hurt me. I felt betrayed.

May GOD judge you.

You have no inkling or shame to your name.

I am in pain like the horse you touch its mane.

No more recording music videos on YouTube.

It's the end of the line that ties you up in twine.

You sure malign.

10/18/19

Beau Soleil = Beautiful Sun

Il fait beau aujourd'hui.= It is beautiful today.

Le soleil avec chaleur de cette des rayons chaleurs le jour.= The sun with heat of the rays of heat of the day.

Beaucoup de bonne journée c'est mieux pour moi.= Many of a good day is better for me.

Je crit que le soleil est il une grande chose de la nature.= I think that the sun is a big thing of nature.

Je suis contente avec la chaleur du jour de l'après- midi.= I am happy with the heat of the day of midday.

J'apprécie beaucoup les rayons de soleil beaucoup toute la journée'.=I appreciate the rays of the sun very much all of the day.

Je dit merci beaucoup à Dieu pour le soleil que fait beau.=I say thank you very much to GOD for the sun is beautiful.

01/31/21

Beach Highway

I was on highway 101 with mom in San Diego County.

I passed by the beaches pristine and sandy.

So goodI forgot too call Christian friend Randy . I enjoyed the fresh air feeling the coolness of the waves. I was hungry but did not eat at

Just me and mom in North County along the coast of California I will boast. Lunch was so delicious with toast. It was perfect Southern Cali weather nice and sunny.

I wish I had a honey. For a woman to meet at the beach for her definitely not a teach . Grom Oceanside to La Jolla punching strong like Oscar De La Hoya.

Slow driving my mom and I were not diving. Into the ocean feeling the motion. I was happy as can be smooth drive you see. Couples not throuples more families,singles in store it was us coming out the door.

02/07/21

Balboa

When I think of a park.

Balboa park comes to mind.

Its little cottages and Hall Of Nations.

The people are friendly and kind.

The House Of Scotland and so many others occupy these cottages.

Taking you around the world so to speak.

Its lawn programs give the park international flavor.

The museums,Japanese Garden,the San Diego Zoo.

So many treasures enveloped in one much more.

For me exhibitions of Art paintings in store.

It is full of surprises with all of its vices.

To me it means a myriad of things.

Gaelic class,and House Of Germany Choir,Folk dancing,clarinet lessons.

This park is a force to be reckoned culturally and in activity beckoned.

Bivo = I Live

Bivo

Ande bive mi almika.= Where does my soul live.

Kon ken tu platika? = With whom do you speak.

Purim lanu nada envanu! = Festival of lots for us nothing in vain!

Yo desho i aspero. = I leave and wait.

Ma agora no te kero. = But now I don't love you.

Korason kito. = Heart brought out.

Ke me afito.= That happen to me.

Yo no so felis.= I am not happy.

En mi payis.= In my country.

Bavajadas=Stupidities

Esto pasando por bavajadas del banko,el rofe, i la eskola.= I am
going through stupidities of the bank,the doctor and the school.

El banko no kere darmi modifikasyon de la devda ma keren
las paras soltanto.= The bank does not want to give me
a modification of the debt but wants money only.

El rofe no sinya los papelikos para kel Departimento di otos di
motores no me desha konsegir mi lisensia de permisyon para
konduizir el oto.= The doctor does not sign the papers for the DMV
doesn't let me get the license of permision to drive the car.

La eskola me da lisiones ke yo no topo bueno komo la aldjebra.=
The school gives me lessons that I don't co good like Algebra.

Yo me syento un hamoriko ke so bovo para ambezarla.=
I feel like a little donkey that is an idiot to learn it.

La bida me da munchas kozas huertes ke no son agradavles.=
Life is giving me many hard things that are not pleasant.

Yo esto andando en la kaleja sin salida.= I am
going into an alley without an exit.

Mi tensyon en mis venas al puntiko ke manko un poko de
Sharope blanko en mi boka.= My tension in my veins to the
little point that lacks a little of white syrup in my mouth.

Kuando va finir estas amudisyones en mi bida presonla.=
When will these curses in my personal life.

Ainde yine mis problemikas no tyenen una solusyon
Baruch Hashem.= Even though it fills my little
problems do not have a solution thank GOD.

Kero topar la salvasyon ve chesed na'ava del DYO
a mi bida entera.=I want to find the salvation and
kindness with love from GOD to my whole life.

No kero bever raki para ulbidar mis problemas.= I don't
want to drink Raisin brandy to forget my problems.

Cosas = Things

Hay muchas cosas que hacer.= There are many things to do. Que es para nacer. = It is for being born. No hay nada que esconder.= There is nothing to hide. Un revés me quita la sed. = A reverse to take away my thirst. Como cortar el césped.= It's like cutting grass. Que me como un aguacate no el zacate.= That I eat an avocado not the grass. Así mismo yo estoy como me voy. = Like at the same time it's like I am going. Es que hay ir a Otay.= It's going to Otay. Nada esta en tarima ni encima.= Nothing is in the stage or above.Entonces oigo las voces de que haga sin una daga!= So I hear the voices of what to do without a dagger! Las cosas no siempre son hermosas.= Things are not always beautiful. Aunque declive hay algo sensible.= Although decline there is something sensible. Todos tenemos cositas igual que las casitas.= We all have little things the same as the little houses.

02/16/23

Cosa Di Vita = Thing of life

La cosa di vita.= The thing of life.

La morte non mi piace.= Death does not please me.

Quante volte la vita perduta.= How many times is life lost.

Gli cose a la morte.= Things to the death.

Io vuoi cose buone per me.= I want good things for me.

Ed la mi famiglia.= and my family.

Molti ricordi belli.= Many good memories.

Ma dove stai il mio vero amore la ragazza preferita?=
But where is my true love the preferred girl?

Facendo il seso sensuale per crescere una nuova
vita come gli bambini?= Making the sensual sex
for growing a new life like the children.

Una parola sol tanto basta!= One word only is enough!
Andiamo al letto amore mio.= Let's go to bed my love.

Dami un baccio e abraciami.= Give me a kiss and hug me.

Dolcemente ed forte.= Sweet and strong.

La vita finisce a le cento anni.=The life finishes at a hundred years.

07/18/11

Colomba=Dove

Quando cado innamorato di lei mia colomba.=
When I fall in love with you my dove.

Lei è venuto d'alto.= You came from above.

A me ho incantato con lei.= To me I am enchanted with you.

Quante maniere di mostrare preoccupazione e la saluto col savoir
faire.= How many ways to show I care and greet you with savoir faire.

Anche se ci sono molti sentieri raggiungerla.= Even
though there are so many paths to reach you.

La grazia di cuore a cuore e chiara.= The grace of heart to heart is clear.

Lei e mio caro.= You are my dear.

Il manzo chiarisce molti ostacoli al nostro amore.=
Steer clear of many obstacles to our love.

Il nostro amore deve essere forte per continuare.=
Our love must be strong for it to go on.

Per esso perseverare e essere maturo.= For it to endure is to be mature.

I sentimenti che abbiamo per l'un l'altro e la cura di felicita.=
The feelings we have for each other is the cure of happiness.

Per noi essere contento nel benessere.= For us to be glad in wellness.

11/19/09

Coca= Coke

Yo quiero mi coca cola.= I love my coca cola.

Un refresco para tomar sola.= It's a refreshment I drink alone.

Yo no me llamo lola.= I am not called Lola.

Así me toca la coca.= That is how the coke touches me.

Para las navidades o días festivos.= For the Christmases or Holidays.

Nos ayuda mantenerse activos.= It helps us to stay active.

La cafeína nos mantiene vivos.=The caffeine keeps us alive.

Quiero mi coca pero no me provoca.= I want
my coke but it does not provoke me.

Sea botella o bote de aluminio no hay querella con un ni~no=
Be it a bottle or a can of aluminium there is no complaint.

Todos alegres con la coca no es color mocha.= Everyone
is happy with the coke; it is not a color mocha.

Es color caramelo no del cielo.= It is the color
of caramel, it is not of the sky.

Yo con la coca me vuelo.= I with the coke I fly.

Para mi es algo rico que en la garganta pica.= It is
something that is rich that in the throat it scratches.

11/24/09

Cuatro Amigos= Four Friends

Um,dois,tres,cuatro amigos.= One ,two ,three, four friends.

Três amigos e um cao.= Three friends and one dog.

Andando,caminhando Agora nós terminamos de caminhar.=
Going,walking now we finish with walking.

Georgia a boa cao pela herva face o popo.= Georgia
a good dog by the grass makes poop.

Nicole levanta eu,Ken e Georgia somos amizades por um dia soleado.=
Nicole picks up I,Ken and Georgia we are friends for a sunny day.

Ficamos em apartamentos com a cruz simbolica.= We
stay in the apartments with a symbolic cross.

Nesse dia acabamos e voltamos ao apartamento.=
That day we finish and return to the apartment.

Falando os três a cão andando também.= Speaking
the three of us the dog is going also.

10/08/19

Commencer L'Amour = Love Begins

Je commence une nouvelle étape de ma vie.= I
am starting a new beginning of my life.

Je désire rencontrer L'amour n'est pas pour un jour.=
I want a meeting love which is not for one day.

Voulez d'une femme Juive ou non Juive seule Dieu savoire.=
I want a Jewish woman or a nonJewish only G-D knows.

La vie commence avec amour après le temps.=
Life begins with love before time.

Je change les choses pour devenir cel bataire a marit entrepreneur .
= I change things for a coming bachelor to a married entrepreneur.

Joyeux pour un famille de femme et fils que je prier a Dieu.=
Joyous for a woman of family and children I ask G-D.

Les mots dans mon coeur et très forts ne sont pas des sports. =
The words in my heart are very strong, they are not for sport.

Allons Y ma chère petit amis pour une fleur de lis.=
Let's go my dear girlfriend for a flower of the lily.

Chacun un jour de faire l'amour.= For such a day to make love.

Toujours prêt, j'allai au parc pour une promenade avec ma jolie blonde.
= All day ready, I go to the park for a stroll with my beautiful blonde.

Suivez la vie doucement non dit Puigdemont.=
Follow life sweetly does not say Puigdemont.

Je préfère un bisou et j 'embrasse mon paramour.=
I prefer a kiss and embrace to my love.

Buvons un café au lait si me plait avec ma chère.= O I
drink a coffee with cream if it pleases my dear.

L'année niveau d'amour me plait beaucoup.=
The year of love it pleases me much.

01/09/20

Climbing The Walls

It seems deep down I am climbing the walls. I keep myself from
hitting the stalls. I can't stand Covid-19 lockdown from town.
I want may freedom to roam and do things. I can't be with my
friends. Everyone everywhere don't you dare is not happy with
this corona virus scare. Self imposed exile in which is not our style.
I feel treated like a child that used to be wild free as can be Today
all activity has ceased. No one is being appeased. I am going crazy
with this pandemic. I feel I am going chronic. Now we are slow not
supersonic. Give me a break to go to the beach or the park only day
light not in the dark. I pray to G-D when will this be over .Banned is
the concert in dover. Climbing the walls disease is catastrophic.

04/15/20

CA Fires of 2020

The fires of 400 are raging throughout Califas. Turning the sun pink
to red to orange. People can breathe in some areas of Northern
California with ash falling on the sidewalks and streets in

San Francisco. People have to stay indoors but luckily we in
Temecula, have not had to be inside still fires to the east of
Riverside County and San Diego counties are raging. It's as
if nature is staging. As far north as Oregon and down to

Southern Cali the fires are blazing. We pray to God for rain to release
the firefighter's strain. Scorching heat smelling like defeat has us
almost beat. Rain is a welcome sign to put out the fires to quell
our heartfelt desires. In G-D we trust California or bust! The rains
will remain out of the storm drain and put out the fires for GOD's
sake don't be a cheapskate. Rebuilding anew on a clean slate.

09/14/20

Cademisiani Siciliani. = Sicilian Academicians

Salutamu a miei amici Siciliani, Videmu un po per andare
la.= I greet my Sicilian friends, I see a little to walk over.

Iu ca l'America comu siti buona. = I here in America like a good sites.

Sira ancura mia famigghia di amici duve si portanu allura a la cita
= It will be my family of friends that go ported still to the city.

Parlanu comu Sicilia ma Iu comi napulitani.= We
speak like Sicily but I like Neopolitan.

10/21/20

Corona Halloween

There were goblins and ghosts but there was no french
toast. This year there were no trick or treaters blast
because of covid-19 they did not come to past.

All the people were having Pizza Parties for their kids.
This Halloween I was slow at watching vids. No more
hustle and bustle noisy children but families at home . I
know Jerome did not roam to the streets to comb.

Covid-19was such a danger the health police sent the health
ranger. It's not Christmas with Jesus in a manger. People still
bought candy for themselves, not elves to keep handy .

I don't know my friends Andy and Mandy. Halloween October
31,2020 was affected by the pandemic. Alas it wasn't very pathetic.

12/03/20

Casa= Home

Eu estou en mi~na casa Ainda non ver o meu renaixer.=I
am in my house even though I don't see my rebirth.

Moito escoito e comou meu froito.= I listen to and eat my fruit.

Cando vou a fora da xanela eu poido oler a canela.= When
I go outside of the window, I can smell the cinnamon.

Casa mi~na eu senti~na moi.= My house I feel much.

Andando a pe e vou que foi.= Going by foot that was.

Nistos dias vamos por visto unha redondela! = In these
days we have gone for a roundabout!? Non as visto
Ay Carmela?= Have you not seen Oh Carmel?

Cando vai facer o meu comer?=When are we going to do my eat?

Todo os dias meu ben querer.= All the days of my good love.

Sozi~no vou ao moi~no.= Alone I go to the mill.

Nesta casa sou un reprandecer cantamos cancions do
meu corazon con emocions.=This house is a splendor
to sing songs of my heart with emotions.

Galiza e onde e mi~na casa bailemos xuntos en na praza.= Galicia
is where is my house where we dance together in the square.

Dou mais felizes son as raizes.= The more happ are the roots.

Xuntos damos abrazos con bicos fraternais d'un aire ancestrais.=
Together we give hugs with fraternal kisses of an ancestral air.

12/03/20

Christmas 2020

Past without a blast. It was a sleepy cold Christmas. Like they say in Spanish Noche Buena sin Pena = Christmas night eve without remorse.

I don't remember doing anything. I s ept throughout the day and night. Without it being in sight. I saw nothing not even Santa Claus or his elves.

I was wondering what I was even dreaming. In this life there is scheming not much presents under all the Christmas trees. My mom had on the Christmas eve.

I did not even call my friend Steve. That's how tired I was. I was not on fire. I did not drink coffee of the wire. Not much hoopla but a quiet humble Christmas cheer without a sneer.

So, there you have it the verdict is out from the spout.

Creatività= Creativity

La creatività nasce di l'anima che luce moltissimo.= The
creativity is born from a soul that lights much.

C una cosa bella creare una cosa nuova e buona. = IT is
a beautiful thing to create a new and good thing.

Faremo felice la creatività dove qualcuno sa sapere tutto e bello.= We
are happy with creativity where one knows everything and is beautiful.

Nessuno sapeva il perché di fare una buona idea che nasce
dietro la catota di uno.= Noone knows the reason for doing
a good idea that is born inside the head of one.

Sempre andiamo troppo in fretta troppo per facere alcuna cosa
di novelta.= We are always in a hurry to do a thing of novelty.

Sappiamo come fiori in un bicchiere di acqua per crescere di
nuovo.= We know like the flowers in a glass of water to grow new.

Soltanto ce una vita piena di cosi nouve per inventare come
una pintura,tecnologia,scienza, televisione, musica, poesia et
cetera.= Only it is a a life full of new things to invent like painting,
technology, science, television, music, poetry et cetera.

Siamo contente di essere studiando per imparare
una creativita dolce e buonissima.= We are happy of
studying to learn a sweet and good creativity.

Andiamo al liceo o universita per fare la creativita. =We are
walking to the college or university to make creativity.

Spontanea tutti gli studenti.= Spontaneous all the students.

01/26/21

Caos Poetico= Poetic Chaos

Hay veces que estoy en un caos poético que no escribo
aunque soy diabetico.= There are times I am in a poetic
chaos because I don't write even though I am diabetic.

Tengo lapsos sufro de falta de inspiración porque se
me acaba la emoción,= I have lapses I suffer from the
lack of inspiration because my emotions finish.

Yo espero y recargar mis baterías como unas pilas. = I wait
and recharge my batteries like if they were piles.

Trato de fomentar mi creatividad en la inmensa mentalidad.=
I try to encourage my creativity in the immense mentality.

Quiero producir poemas de todos los temas para
mí son los lemas.=I want to produce my poems
of all the themes for my sound of slogans.

Sacarlos a flote mi alma y corazón sin perder la razon.= To
bring them out my soul and heart without losing reason.

Este caos limita mi poesía cada dia.= This
chaos limits my poetry each day.

Falta de imaginación reinventarme es mi sensación.= The
lack of imagination to reinvent myself is a sensation.

Poderme hacer valer es mi convence᠆ hecho adelante
Dios mediante.= To make myself worth is to convince
me what is done before GOD willing.

Como curar mi caos poético darme un vaje a México.= How
to heal my poetic chaos to give myself a trip to Mexico.

Ir hacia la naturaleza es para mi una realeza.=
Go toward nature is my royalty.

De tanto trabajo y esfuerzo me gano las regalias dia a dia.=From
so much work and effort I win my royalties day to day.

Espero en Dios hacia el alzo mi voz que me quita la poética tos.= I wait in GOD toward raising my voice and take away the poetic cough.

Caos poético esta ya nomas en el cibernetico.= Poetic chaos is now in the cybernetic.

02/07/21

Church

I look forward to Tuesdays since I go with
mom to Justin's grandmas house.

Once I get there mom drops me off. Justin,granny and I eat and chat.

After sometime from Temecula to Miramesa
its on to Santee for church.

But we go to pick up James in San Diego Downtown and another
person it used to be Tiffany Rose. No we don't strike a pose.

I sit and relax but don't dose. We hear Christian music which is not
acoustic. We get to Jason and Sashas even though I'm not pasha.

We meet ,greet, hug and shake hands with people who
arrive. I am stoked not provoked to not take a dive.

We sing, read bible and pray for GOD we strive. It
lasts till late without missing a beat I syncopate. Then
we leave without my pet peave to home.

Justin and I drop off James and Tiff then we roam from San
Diego to Temecula sans an if. I get back to the house thank God
no mouse.Justin takes off to his grandmothers in Miramesa.

He calls me to let me know he made it not taking condesa.

02/08/21

Chanuka=Hanukah

Ande vo ir para chanukia.= Where will I go for the Hanukiah.

Es mi bida espartida sin Keila.= It is my life
dispersed without a synagogue.

Ya no tengo un rabino para selebrarla ni la teva.= I
don't have a rabbi to celebrate nor the podium.

Para dizir sheva sheva sheva.= To say seven seven seven.

Bivo komo sekularo no djidio.= I live like a secular not a Jew.

Syempre vo para mudar or ir a eshpital.= Always
I go to move or go to the hospital.

Como Vai?=How Goes It?

Como vai amigo meu?= How goes it my friend?

Ainda estao em um chao.=Still I am in a plain.

Como um cavaleiro entre as montanhas.=Like
a knight between the mountains.

Cheias das vacas sempre afora em ervas verdes.=Full
of cows always outside in green herbage.

Os pastos que comeu as animais.=The pastures that the animals eat.

A Borboleta voando em o ar.= The butterfly flying in the air.

Trabalhando forte os vaquieros.=Working strong the cowherds.

Que deixam o sudor do corpo fatigados de labrada.=That
leave the sweat of the body fatigued from the labround.

O labor do dia a noite a fronte dos montes.= The
work of day a night in front of the mountains.

Pela brisa do vento cantando as cancoes de povo.= Of the
breeze of the wind singing the songs of the nation.

Da gente pequena que nao tem muito dinheiro.=
Of the people that don't have much money.

Comencar de Novo=Start A New

Eu tenho que mudar do povo de Temecula a cidade do San Diego.= I have to move from the town of Temecula to the city of San Diego.

Eu quero voltar fazer o mesmo Ysmael de antes mais que nada estar com meus paes e amizades.=I want to become the same Ysmael of before more than anything to be with my parents and friends.

Voltar a Michm,Escola de Adultos e Visões.= Return to Michm,Adult school and Visions.

Comencar de Novo pra um encontro e fazer minha felicidade uma realidade.= To start a new meeting and make my happiness a reality.

Desquecer todo que foi o ano inteiro de Junho 2008 a Junho 2009.= Forget everything that was the entire year of June 2008 to June 2009.

Estar em paz com Deus e minha alma sempre avante com na frente forte.= To be at peace with GOD and my soul always advanced with the strong face.'

Deijar todo o pasado atras no mais.= Leave everything the past behind only.

Disquecer todo que foi mau pra mim.=Forget everything that was bad for me.

Como Vai?=How Goes It?

Como vai amigo meu?= How goes it my friend?

Ainda estao em um chao.=Still I am in a plain.

Como um cavaleiro entre as montanhas.=Like
a knight between the mountains.

Cheias das vacas sempre afora em ervas verdes.=Full
of cows always outside in green herbage.

Os pastos que comeu as animais.=The pastures that the animals eat.

A Borboleta voando em o ar.= The butterfly flying in the air.

Trabalhando forte os vaquieros.=Working strong the cowherds.

Que deixam o sudor do corpo fatigados de labrada.=That
leave the sweat of the body fatigued from the labround.

O labor do dia a noite a fronte dos montes.= The
work of day a night in front of the mountains.

Pela brisa do vento cantando as cancoes de povo.= Of the
breeze of the wind singing the songs of the nation.

Da gente pequena que nao tem muito dinheiro.=
Of the people that don't have much money.

Deseo = Desire

Yo deseo un amor verdadero más que no sea el clero. = I want a real love but not the clergy. Judío y Moro soy de Espa~na vengo y voy. = Jewish and Moor I am from Spain I come and I go. Anhelando mujer Sefardita o Mora.= Desiring a Sephardic or Moorish women. Quiero que me conquiste el corazón sin perder la razón.= I want her to conquer my heart without losing the reason. Lo quiero fácil sin problemon.= I want it easy without a huge problem. Yo no me llamo Ramon.= I am not called Raymond. Soy Ysmael no Miguel.= I am Ysmael not Michael. Quiero ser como mi Padre Abram con una Caldea y Egipcia mas moderna Judía y Arabe.= I want to be like my Father Abraham with a Chaldean and an Egyptian but m more modern a Jewess and Arabic woman. Mi deseo arde mucho más dela cuenta no tomo jarabe.= My Ardent desire much more is that I don't take syrup.

02/25/23

Doom

It's gloom and doom. The rain is coming like a zoom. Depression gray and stays. The clouds are not black or white but in between know what I mean? Not on site. So many shades of gray. I don't want to play. The fog in the bog will not walk the dog.It is raining affecting my mood that I don't want food.We have to stay indoors but not sleep on floors. As I can say stay away in the house. I need a cat to kill the mouse. For the rain is leaving me in pain due to the doom. As if I am buried in my tomb. At night it's not so bright.

03/14/23

Disconnected

Sometimes I feel disconnected from my family or friends.

My relatives don't answer me or if they do they don't tell me
I'm tired or busy or I have to rest and get ready for work.

I can't talk now if they do talk to me when I call them back and stab
me by complaining about me to my younger sister or my mom.

I don't visit or call them anymore.

My friends live far from me. Usually we have nothing to
talk about and as a result they don't always call me.

I feel disconnected from society and my community.

Temecula is conservative and it is hard for me to make friends.

They are very close minded.

I'm not Christian Catholic or Protestant but Jewish
it's even harder for me to socialize with them.

Jewish people are open and warm only to friends from
childhood or at work and members of the family.

I am isolated even from the Jewish community.

Being a disabled vet and single at 48 I am seen as a pariah.

No wife or girlfriend and kids. Some think I'm
gay without asking me directly.

I feel the disconnect no matter what.

I'm not in college,university,a career or a job.

Therefore people do not relate to me.
How will my life change GOD?

I want a solution not a disconnect .
When will there be my light at the end of the tunnel?
I have to keep busy to keep from losing it.
I suffer in silence.
I am disconnected.
10/12/19

Dia De Los Muertos= Day Of The Dead

Dia de los muertos se aproxima Noviembre.= Day
of the dead is approximating November.

Tiempo de copal y cempasuchil.= Time of copal incense and mary gold.

Pan dulce de cadáver muerto.= Sweet bread of dead cadáver.

Los tiempos prehispánicos con flautas y tambores=
The prehispanic times with flutes and drums.

Los Aztecas y sen~ores.= The Aztecs and the lords.

Tiempos del más allá de los ancestros.= Times
of the beyond of our ancestors.

El hilo umbilical de nuestros abuelos.= The
umbilical cord of our grandfathers.

Un ciclo de la vida un suspiro.= A cycle of life is a sigh.

Así es como acontecen los tiempos.= That is how times occur.

Muchos platillos típicos Mexicanos como Mole Pipián y
velas prendidas con los altares.= Many typical Mexican
dishes like Mole Pipian and candles lit with altars.

Fotos de nuestra familia visitas a las iglesias, sinagogas o mezquitas
según nuestros credos.= Pictures of our family visits to the
churches,synagogues or mosques according to our creeds.

El tiempo para reflexionar en el otoño.= It's
the time to reflect on the fall.

Comiendo maíz o tamales sin los lodazales.= Eating
corn or tamales without the landslides.

10/25/19

Dias De Reflexão = Days of Reflection

Agora acho em minha vida que foi São Tiago. =
Now I think in my life that was San Diego.

Sempre penso em bom tempo de outono e inverno. = I
always think in the good times of autumn and fall.

Sempre tem tempo pra refletir. = There is time to reflect.

Adoro as cores preto do sezon ainda vou.= I adore the
dark colors of the season even though I go.

Achando que fazer nadinha mas pra isso acontecer. =
Thinking of what to do nothing more for that to happen.

Primeiro os tempos eu lembro que foi. = First
the times I remember that were.

Agora moro em Temecula. = Now I live in Temecula.

Eu refleti que vai ser a vida pra mim. = I
reflect of what will life be for me.

Ninguém sabe o futuro só Deus no mais.= No
one knows the future, only God.

Até logo São Tiago quando eu voltar.= See you
later San Diego when will I return.

Senti-me contento andando do La Jolla a Povo Velho pra Chula
Vista com meu cunhado e irmã.= I feel content going from La Jolla
to Old Town for Chula Vista with my brother-in-law and sister.

10/25/19

49

Do I Love Myself

I am ambivalent concerning me because of my weight.
It's taken time for me to love myself. I don't like being
overweight. I feel I would look younger if I were skinny.

It has taken a long time for me to love myself. I must affirm I am
tanned and handsome to look at in spite of my heaviness. For
men and women to be attracted to me sexually would be an
infusion of self-esteem validation. A physical attraction sensation.
I don't want negative depravation. They say beauty is in the eye
of the beholder confidence would make me boulder. If people
think I'm ugly it's a cold shoulder. I need to realize there is more
to me than meets the eye. Physical endorphins fuel my high.
I guess auto love for me is worth a try. Do I love myself.

04/15/20

Despair

Out of despair is too much to bear. I drove around the town, knowing
hardly anyone. Desolation is rampant. When will we be normal again.
Idrove for a spin. I eat out at the park before it gets dark. I called my
friend. He was not waiting at the end. I left mom at home in order for
me to roam. I can't stand the isolation coming through the nation. It's
like being asleep without a little bo peep. I can't take it anymore back
to normal to settle the score. Only so much out the door it's like getting
up from a snore. When will the nightmare end to my delight, not
things out of spite. 2020 is hindsight. When will things return to where
they were? It's like wishing upon a star. God help me pull through
anger and spit to a hew. Normal is far gone just like singing a song.

05/18/20

Deseo = Desire

Yo deseo un amor verdadero más que no sea el clero. = I want a real love but not the clergy. Judío y Moro soy de Espa~na vengo y voy. = Jewish and Moor I am from Spain I come and I go. Anhelando mujer Sefardita o Mora.= Desiring a Sephardic or Moorish women. Quiero que me conquiste el corazón sin perder la razón.= I want her to conquer my heart without losing the reason. Lo quiero fácil sin problemon.= I want it easy without a huge problem. Yo no me llamo Ramon.= I am not called Raymond. Soy Ysmael no Miguel.= I am Ysmael not Michael. Quiero ser como mi Padre Abram con una Caldea y Egipcia mas moderna Judía y Arabe.= I want to be like my Father Abraham with a Chaldean and an Egyptian out m more modern a Jewess and Arabic woman. Mi deseo arde mucho más dela cuenta no tomo jarabe.= My Ardent desire much more is that I don't take syrup.

02/25/23

Division

La politique et Religion divisee' la famille.=
Politics and religious divide the family.

Ceci est un malaise dans la vie quotidienne.=
It is a malady of the daily life.

Tout le monde non faire la paix ce bataillé pour tout.=All of
the world doesn't make peace to battle for everything.

je crois que non est il très bonne pour la salut de les personne.=
I think it is not very good for the health of the person.

Je dirai si vous voulez la paix non discutée' religion ou politique
parce que la famille disparaît et disparaît avec le sujet.=I say
if you want peace don't discuss religion or politics because
family disappears and disappears with the subject.

Je recommande de parler du climat, des sports ,la musique
pour ne pas être détesté avec nous.=I recommend talking
about climate, sports and music so as not to hate us.

Se fomente' une environnement de guerre constant vis à vis
de la religion et de la politique.= It fomented one environment
of war constantly face to face of religion and of politics.

Je haine la situation pour ma famille s' irrite considerablement.=I
hate the situation because my family irritates considerably.

Tout le monde n'accorde pas le même sujet pacifiquement.=
Everybody does not agree with the same subjects peacefully.

Préfère' laisser la controverse' dans la division avec la
famille ou personne.= I prefer to let the controversy
in the division with my family or person.

Je dis non aux choses disparues.=I say no to the things that disappear.

09/05/2020

Dia De los Muertos = Day of the Dead

Mom made meat dishes to placate my dead cads wishes. Mexican day of the dead I have not lost my own head. Upstairs, downstairs I tread without thinking ahead. No cempasuchil or pictures of my dead or fruit offering on the table no not one of my aunts is called Mable. We greet our thanks to GOD. We are stable. Marigolds without their folds is what has made me bold. Precolumbian celebrates the Mesoamericans' sensation of Mexico's advanced native civilizations. In the U.S we celebrate across the nation. It's with my mom that I have these days Nov 1st and 2nd for a conversation. But in Spain it's all souls day here in the United States it is a segue from Halloween. Now you know what I mean. Day of the dead.

12/03/20

Days

The days go by like water five years dead my father. I see through many a time a changing the water is wading.

It seems time does not stand still however it must, it will. With covid-19 pandemic much in life has stopped like a picture that has been cropped. I see the writing on the wall society taken a big fall.

We all are trying to recover from the corona virus it makes me think of King Cyrus. I am taken aback by the slow end of things stack. Days that go by won't return that have taken a sharp turn.

To many could of, would of but didn't. A last that is life full of strife. I am single no wife. Days that come and go it will make you steal the show. Everything happens for a reason that is time and a season.

01/19/21

Diya De San Valentino= Valentines Day

Todos endjuntos kada ken kon su kada kual.
= All together each with his own.

Konfitura solikos en sus parejas.= Candy alone with its pairs.

Kontentes los dos en braso en braso djuntos.=
Happy arm in arm just the two together.

Fuites un santo ke influyensyastes el diya del namorado de las parejas
de kidushin kon munchas rozas.= You were a saint who influenced
the day of the lovers in pairs to get married with many roses.

Mozotros asperamos tener muestra almikabudjuk.=
We await for our twin soul.

La flechada yega en una tadrada d'amor la senyorika
i el novyo.= The cupids arrow comes in a afternoon
of love of the misses and her boyfriend.

Munchas kartikas se embiyan kon bonbonikos el Febrayo
14.= Many cards are sent with candy on February 14.

Origino la selesbrasyon kon un papaz katoliko un papa de la chorcha
ande las parejas espozadas kon beraha de la iglesya.= It originated
with the celebration of a catholic pope a priest with all the flock
where with the married couples and blessings of the church.

Las parejikas salen ahuera de braso en braso kon konfit, i flores de roz.=
The couples come outside arm in arm with candy and pink flowers.

Agora bivimos el diya namorozos endjuntos felises i kolay.=
Now we live the day in love together happy and easy.

Ande mi i mi nefesh budjukes estamos bezandomos
la boka kon magrana.= Where I and my twin soul is
kissing us with the mouth and a pomegranate.

02/14/21

Dia Kema=Day That Burns

Ke dia tan odyozo nada para mi orozo.=What
a hateful day nothing happy for me.

Alumbre kema komo ferose diyadema.= Alight
it burns like a ferocious diadem.

No kontamos kon la eskema.=We do not tell with a scheme.

De buto al tino.= From the aim to memory.

No es un tema.= It is not a theme.

Ya me vino el lema.= It came to me the watchword.

Kazas, atadishos keman.= Houses, ligations burn.

Al DIO alto teman.= To GOD most high fear.

Ke pekados azimos tyempos bashos pasimos.= What
sins have we committed low times we passed.

Diya de Grasyas= Day Of Thanks

Munchos no saven la vedra.= Many don't know the truth.

Sobre ke yay muncho rengrasyar al DIO.=
Over there is much to thank GOD.

Ke mos salvo del olokausto.= He saved us from the holocaust.

La Shoa vino a muncho Selaniklis i Monastirlis ansi komo altros
Sefardim de los Balkanes.= The holocaust came to many Saloniklis
and Monastirlis even like other Sephardim of the Balkans.

Libero a moztrosh en Aushvitz.= They freed us in Auswitz.

Kuando vinyeron los Amerikanos a la Almanya.=
When the Americans came to Germany.

Mujeres,ombres i fijos de Fransia,Beldjika i Olanda.=
Women,men and children of France,Belgium and Holland.

Los kapos de la shoa en sus komandas.= The capos
of the holocaust in thier commands.

Fizyeron lavoros kruelos a todos ladino avlantes.= They
made them do cruel labor to all the Ladino Speakers.

En una banda kon los non-Sefardim Jdudios.= In
a band with the non-Sephardic Jews.

Guerearon la djente komo partisanos en la guera.=
The people fought like partisans in the war.

Los ke se skaparon de los kampos de la muerte.=
The ones that escaped the death camps.

En Makedonya avia una Partisana Gavriela Ovadia.= In
Macedonia there was a partisan Gabriela Ovadia.

Dia Do Dar Graca=Day Of Giving Thanks

Dia pra mim natural.= Day for me natural.

Obrigado pela vida.= Thankful for life.

Porque todo e dificil.=Because everything is difficult.

Nadinha facil pra viver.= Nothing easy to live.

Hoje e dia da Graca por DEUS.=Today is Day of Thanks for GOD.

Que do isto a no mundo enteiro.= What of this to the whole world.

Comeu indianas tambem mirtas em Estados Unidos que Brasil.=We eat the turkies also the blueberries in the United States than Brazil.

Deixa todo em paz.= leaves everything in peace.

Sempre estar com sua familha e amizade.= Always to be with ones family and friends.

Dancando por na musica na noite em na paz.= Dancing for the music in the night in the peace.

Eu = I

Eu estou em minha terra natal, tudo isso é bom. Comigo vou mais porque eu sou. Pra mim estou lembrando os passos que estou passando. Quando lembro minha chikes foi sem alegria. Há muito tempo eu perdi por meu descontento, isto foi meu lamento. Nadinha eu bebi uma caipirinha limão, açúcar e cachaça com gelo. Comendo feijoada com farofa a lume cozinha tudo bom cachaça e um rom.= I am in my native land ,everything is good. With me I go more because I am. For me remembering the steps I am passing. When I remember my childhood was without happiness. It has been a long time since I lost my discontent, this was my lament. I drink Caipirinha lemon, sugar, and cachaca with ice. Eating Feijoada with farofa to the flame of the kitchen all with one cachaca and a rum.

02/04/23

El Mar = The Sea

El mar lleno de almejas y peces.= The sea is full of clams and fish. Un pescado multicolor.= A multi colored fish. Es el resplendor.= It is splendor. Solo pesco por un día para mi señor. =I only wish for one for my lord. Niveles sin cebeles que no tienen percebes.= The levels without cybeles do not have barnacles. Las delicias del Océano Atlántico cerca de Galicia.= The delicacies of the Atlantic Ocean near Galicia. A coci~na Galega que mais da.= The Galician kitchen what more gives. O corazón que volta que acha.= The heart that returns that thinks. Calquer muller ter escoitar moito comer o froito que o cantiga escoito.=Any woman that has to listen much eat the fruit that the song I hear. Asi se fala en Galiza.= That is how its spoken in Galicia.. Manjares de la Espa~na Noroeste la azul celeste que le cueste. = Delicacies of Northeastern Spain the blue celestial may it cost. Como va el pez que pesque. = Like the fish that I caught. El sol es brillante en cada instante. = The sun is bright in each instant. Todo es Dios mediante. = Everything is God be willing. Siete percebes y cuatro pescados con sus hados. = Seven barnacles and four fish with thier fates.

02/26/23

El Gato De Visiones= The Cat Of Visions

Este gato tiene muchos nombres que todos le llamamos en visiones.= This cat has many names that we all call him at visions. Unos le dicen Henry, yo le digo pardo el varon o spots the tom cat.= Some call him Henry, I call him dark the male or spots the tom cat.

No se como le llaman los demas ?Patches?= I don't know what the others call him. Patches?

'Este gato tiene genio es muy cari~noso pero no ra~noso.= This cat is a genuine and is very loving but mangy.

Todos abrazamos o lo levantamos.=We all embrace the cat or pick him up.

Todos nosotros queremos al gato mejor que un pato.= We all like him better than a duck.

Siempre lo miramos al rato.= We always see him a later.

Va y viene pero no nos retiene.= He comes and goes but he doesn't reta n us.

El es blanco pero pardos escuras esta gordo y grande.= He is white but dark he's fat and big.

Estara con nosotros hasta que Dios mande.= He will be with us till God calls him.

Es definitivamente curioso e amoroso Henry.= He is definately curious and loving Henry.

11/18/09

Esta Lluvia Temporal = The Temporary Rain

Esta lluvia temporal ojala que la próxima vez no sea tan severa más placentera.= This temporary rain I hope that the next time it will not be so severe more pleasant.

Es pero no más siga como lodazales piedras etcétera cierran los caminos.= It is but no more following the landslides rocks etcetera that closes the roads.

A dos parientes les pasó eso.= To two relatives that happened.

Santa Bárbara y San Diego son dónde vienen para atrás a Texas.= Santa Barbara and San Diego are where they go back to Texas.

No se cuando volveran solo el Dio lo sabrán no es así es la vida unos van otros vienen.= I don't know when they will return only God knows it is not how life is some go others come.

02/05/19

Eu sinto = I feel

Eu sinto d'entro minha alma a paz da calma.=I
feel inside my soul the peace of calm.

Eu tenho minha família ainda que faço muito trabalho.=
I have my family even though I do much work.

O verão e o mês de julho.= Summer is the month of July.

Porque escrever meus sentimentos do meu coração cheio de
emoção. = Why write my feelings of my heart full of emotion.

Jugando com meu livro como se fosse brinquedo não
disque.=Playing with my book like it were a toy doesn't forget.

O dia já passou o céu cinza e começa a tarde. = The
day has passed, the sky is gray and it starts late.

Depois da chuva vem a noite.= After the rain comes the night.

Temecula rodeada das montanhas e das palmeiras.=
Temecula surrounded by mountains and palms.

Comendo e bebendo toda tarde enteira.= Eating
and drinking all the entire afternoon.

Terminado o jantar da Taco Bell.= Finishing dinner from Taco Bell.

Não sinto terrível a tarde em vez de comer.= I don't
feel terrible the afternoon instead of eating.

Dr Pepper quero beber não trocar meu parecer.= Dr
Pepper I want to drink not to change my viewpoint.

Bejo os automóveis passar sem meus pés andar.= I
see the cars pass without my feet walking.

As avenidas são tão grandes ou lugares amáveis.= The
avenues are very big the places are friendly.

Todo bom a gente é incrível.= Everything
good the people are incredible.

Muito bom pra mim.= Very good for me.

01/21/20

Este Diya De Hanukia=This Day of Chanukah Menorah

Este diya agora embiyamos a la sinyora un buto.=This
day now we send the lady an objective.

Al Dio grasyas no es un barambuto. = To
G-D thanks it is not a bogeyman.

Yo so sefardi el Dio lo kisho ansi.= I am Sephardic G-D wanted it to be.

Es komo yo digo mersi.= It's like I say thank you.

Kolay i difisil no me gosta el trushil.= Easy
and difficult. I don't like parsley.

Munchas presonas non ke vemos las kandelas mozotros
ensenderemos. = Many people that don't see the candles we light up.

Hanuka empesa ainda los ocho diyas.= Chanukah starts the eight days.

Birmuelikos i chokolata beveremos. = Matzah
fritters and chocolate we drink.

Munchas hanukiyot fraguamos.= Many hanukiahs we build.

Biva el Dio alegres no enlutamos solo soriza i felisida.= Long
live G-D happy we mourn not only smile and happiness.

Kantigas de hanuka yo kanti djogaremos naipes kon velunta.=
Chanukah songs I sang and played with Spanish cards with good will.

Bombonikos de chokolata i chai. = Chocolate candies and tea.

Solo ochos regalos i no chai. = Only eight presents and no life.

Dar a la karidad parnasa de komer i non vino ke lamber.= Give
to charity staples of livelihood to eat and not wine to lick.

12/03/20

Esperando Sexo=Waiting For Sex

Esperando para ir hacer el sexo.= Waiting to go to do sex.

Yo espero los cuerpos desnudos blancos.=I
wait for the naked white bodies.

Dotados yenas como la fruta.= They are well endowed like the fruit.

Hacer follar y tocar

Fyesta De Frutas = Feast Of Fruits

Tu Bish Vat ya paso kuatro yayin tomamos de vino blanko i korolado. =
Tu Bish Vat already passed four wine we drink of white and red wine.

Agora las frutas de Yisrael komimos
azeytunas,figos,magranas,sheftali,portokal i uvas de Eretz Yisrael.=
Now the fruits of Israel we eat olives,figs,pomegranates,peach,orange
and grapes of the Land of Israel.

El anyo Muevo de los arvoles almendra,avramila,mansana tambyen
komemos muncho asta artarnos.=The new year of the trees,
Almond,plum,apple also we eat them much to fill ourselves.

Mozotros semos muy kontentes fasta muzika tanyemos.=
We are very happy even music we play.

03/20

Fala Comigo Hoxe=Talk To Me Today

Eu vou ou parque ainda pra cami~nar por o lago.= I
go to the park even though to walk by a lake.

A comer primeiro en Mc Donalds depois andar en meu
coche.=First to eat at MC Donalds then go in my car.

Cantando da mi~na nai onten cando chegei moito do
que pensei.=I was singing of my mother yesterday
when I came very close of what I was thinking.

Achando moi do que acho ninguen sabe que pasa por mi~na
cabeza dentro meu corazon.= Thinking much of what I think
no one knows what goes through my head or in my heart.

Vejo xente dar os pasos pelo lago.= I see people give steps by the lake.

Eu vei os patos ,cans e as familias en a tarde.= I see the
ducks, dogs and families in the evening or afternoon.

Moito do que pensar meu ben.= Much that
I have to think about my good.

CoronaVirus e mais perigozo do que pensa porque
esta no ar.= CoronaVirus and is more dangerous
than what you think because it's in the air.

O ceu azul conte~ne os primeiros brotes da virus.=
The blue sky has the first shoots of the virus.

Todos os te~nemos que ficar con cuidado moito perigo.=
We all have to with great care for there is much danger.

Ainda lembro nestos tempos dificeis pra min e nossa familia.= Even
though I remember these difficult times for me and our family.

03/23/20

Feliz Aniversario=Happy Anniversary

Que lindo saber Tio Ricardo y Tia Hilda su aniversario 55
de casados.=How beautiful to know Uncle Richard and
Aunt Hilda your 55th anniversary of marriage.

Que Dios los bendiga siempre colmados de bendiciones.=
May G-D bless you always full of blessings.

Rodeados de sus hijos nietos y bisnietos todos juntos
felices.= Surrounded by your children, grandchildren
and greatgrandchildren all together happy.

Me da mucha esperanza ver juntos todavia.= It gives
me much hope to see you together still.

No lo puedo creer despues de pasar por muchas cosas
y yo cumpli mis 49 a~nos.= I can't believe it after many
things have passed and I completed my 49 years.

Sigo soltero buscando mi pareja.= I'm single
still looking for my other half.

Pero me dan ilusion de estar con alguien.= But you
give me the illusion of being with someone.

Yo tambien espero celebrar un aniversario semejante y seguir p'alante.
= I too look forward to celebrate a similar anniversary and go forward.

La vida da muchas vueltas se sufre mucho pero ustedes siguen
juntos son una bendicion para mi.= Life gives many turns and you
suffer much but you continue together you are a blessing to me.

Si yo quiero mucho a mis tios porque son mi sangre.= I love
you much my aunt and uncle because you are my blood.

Ellos me ganaron el cari~no asi que le doy gracias a Dios por ellos
dos.=They have won my affection that I give thanks to G-D for them two.

Mi tio me da consejos y mi tia me da cari~no yo se que
ellos me quieren a mi.= My uncle gives me advice and my
aunt gives me affection I know that they love me.

05/01/20

Facemu=That We do

Vulisu unu kasteddu pir caminata d'un kavaddu.=
I want a castle for a walk of a horse.

Duvi andatu Pirandello in Palermu.= Where
Pirandello walked in Palermo.

Doppu andiammu pirchi parratu il dialettu Sicilianu.=
Later we walk because I speak the Sicilian dialect.

Me manca la practica per parlato questo dialetto.= I
lack the practice of having spoken this dialect.

Caro dal mio cuore dietro l'anima mia .=
Dear to my heart inside my soul.

Che cosa sia per me la nostalgia.=For that is a nostalgia for me.

Floresikas Mavis Blu= Blue Little Flowers

Fn el enverano salen las floresikas mavis blu.= In the
summer the blue little flowers come out.

Ke me azen pensar en el sielo blue.= That
make me think of the blue sky.

Una kolor komo la mar para mi komo ver la agua.= A
color like the sea for me like seeing the water.

Para mi es el favorito mi esprito bola en mavi.= For
me it is the favorite my spirit flys in blue.

Yo penso en en este kolor blu.= I think in the blue color.

Las floresikas mavis blu son una kolor fresko.=
The little blue flowers are a fresh color.

Ke dan ayre de golor bueno es kolor maskulino.= That
give air of good smell it is a masculine color.

Ke esta en tino todo me inspira el blu.= This is what I
have in mind everything inspires me the blue.

Komo un ayre alimpiado puro.= Like a clean pure air.

Suave no blando i duro.= It is soft not bland and hard.

Veo un prado yeno de flores blu.= I see a
meadow full of blue flowers.

Ma floresikas en una mabulla mavi me puedo pedrer.=
But little flowers in a blue deluge I can get lost in.

Parfumado de golor dulse ansi komo un miyel blu.=
Perfumed of sweet smell like a blue honey.

Estas floresikas las tyenes tu es shalom para mi kuando
veygo estas floresikas.= This little flowers you have them
is peace for me when I see this little flowers.

Me imajino ver a los ojos de una mujer.= I
imagine seeing her eyes of the woman.

Sus ojos mavis son komo estas floresikas.=
Her blue eyes are like these flowers.

Me enamoro de las floresikas blu para mi las floresikas
mavi blu son todo esto.= I fall in love with the blue little
flowers for me the blue little flowers are all this.

Fruchiguari Mi Bida = Multiply My Life

Fruchiguari mi bida komo el ashugar.= Multiply my life like the dowry.

La bida para mi kerida loar.=The life for my beloved give thanks.

Agora ke vo fazer kadal dia de mi bida.= Now
I am going to do each day of my life

No kero enfasar ni enflamar la yama de mi esensya.= I don't
want to erase nor inflame the spark of my essence.

El chacham ke me gia de noche i dia faze una maraviya. = The
wise one that guides me night and day makes a marvel

Todo esto kontente porke lo negro desho mi mente. =
Everything I am content that the wicked has left my mind.

Enfasado el pasado i un muevo hal para bivir mijor enflamado de amor.
= The past erased and a new state of living better inflamed of love.

Yo kero goler el golor de la flor.= I want to smell the smell of the flower.

El guesmo de portokal i hasmin en la guerta de los hortolanos.=The
rind of the orange and jasmine in the garden of the gardeners.

Me da esperansa para un porvenir mijor.=It
gives me hope for a better future.

Inshala el DIO i la endevina lo auguren pronto.=GOD willing
that GOD and the fortuneteller wil predict soon.

Fruchiguari mi bida el hupa de fija i su katan para dar kidushin
kon bendisyones.= Multiply my life the wedding canopy of
daughter and her groom to nuptial blessings of blessings.

Floresikas Mavis Blu= Blue Little Flowers

Fn el enverano salen las floresikas mavis blu.= In the
summer the blue little flowers come out.

Ke me azen pensar en el sielo blue.= That
make me think of the blue sky.

Una kolor komo la mar para mi komo ver la agua.= A
color like the sea for me like seeing the water.

Para mi es el favorito mi esprito bola en mavi.= For
me it is the favorite my spirit flys in blue.

Yo penso en en este kolor blu.= I think in the blue color.

Las floresikas mavis blu son una kolor fresko.=
The little blue flowers are a fresh color.

Ke dan ayre de golor bueno es kolor maskulino.= That
give air of good smell it is a masculine color.

Ke esta en tino todo me inspira el blu.= This is what I
have in mind everything inspires me the blue.

Komo un ayre alimpiado puro.= Like a clean pure air.

Suave no blando i duro.= It is soft not bland and hard.

Veo un prado yeno de flores blu.= I see a
meadow full of blue flowers.

Ma floresikas en una mabulla mavi me puedo pedrer.=
But little flowers in a blue deluge I can get lost in.

Parfumado de golor dulse ansi komo un miyel blu.=
Perfumed of sweet smell like a blue honey.

Estas floresikas las tyenes tu es shalom para mi kuando
veygo estas floresikas.= This little flowers you have them
is peace for me when I see this little flowers.

Me imajino ver a los ojos de una mujer.= I
imagine seeing her eyes of the woman.

Sus ojos mavis son komo estas floresikas.=
Her blue eyes are like these flowers.

Me enamoro de las floresikas blu para mi las floresikas
mavi blu son todo esto.= I fall in love with the blue little
flowers for me the blue little flowers are all this.

Grandi O Piccolo = Big Or Small

Grandi o piccolo io prego a Dio grazie per il villaggio o la citta.=
Big or small I pray to GOD thanks for the village or city.

La vita davanti dolce o no ma non caspita. = Life
advances sweet or no but not a pity.

Io esisto per vivere molto felice.= I exist to live very happily.

No faccio senza abbraccio e bacio.= I don't
do without hugging and kissing.

Scoperto dove il vero amore che stai dietro il cuore.= I
discover where the real love is inside the heart.

Una donna ed un signore. A woman and a man.

Supra tutto non dico niente senza intelligenza. = Overall
I don't say anything without intelligence.

Come un viaggio in agenzia.= Like a voyage in an agency.

La vita continua sulla forza del destino su Albertino. =
Life continues with force of destiny with Albert.

Canta una canzone d'amore come odori la fiore.=
Sing a song of love to smell the flowers.

Una bella signora mi chiami ancora.= A beautiful lady that calls me still.

Vedere la vita della nostra comunità.=I see the life of our community.

Parliamo francese a un mese dal Piemonte.= We
speak French in the month of the Piedmonte.

Allora andiamo in fretta fra le due Io e Martineta.= Now
we go in a hurry the two of us, I and Martineta.

Temecula e la mia citta allora è una incantevole signora.=
Temecula is my city now and an enchanting lady.

Io arrivo per volare al cielo blu sul la giu.= I
arrive to fly to the sky blue below.

01/21/20

72

Gray Clouds

I see the gray clouds invested like shrouds. Heavy rain is approaching to flood the heavens with water. It's flood the heavens with water

It's like I'm getting ready to sputter. I can feel the cold air from yesteryear. Temperatures coming down with no barking hound. The sun is no where to be seen from me fat to lean. I drink my hot coffee with vanilla bean. No clear skies its if I forgot the dyes. Gray clouds what are they a dark shadow sways. The sun filters somewhat through but I can smell the rain drop dew. I can't see creatures not even a shrew. Who knew how you do. I see the trees, plants and grass some fruit and flowers I pass. The different shade of gray not overlooking the bay. The contrast silhouette recalls when I met my pet. I await the rain with gray clouds and no pain.

04/12/20

Ground Hog Day

The ground hog signals the beginning of Spring.
The end winter means longer days.

More sunny weather instead of the cold rains. No more icy weather but pure warmth. Flowers and fruits bloom including roses.

The animals come out of hibernation like the bears. I see better days ahead of pure joy with plenty of play.

02/02/21

Good Looking Person

A gorgeous person looked my way captivating me with its sway.

Good looking and blonde.

Blessed in the right places beyond.

Well endowed sexy to look upon.

Ignoring me pretending not letting on.

Having enticing goods.

But not my neck of the woods.

A tease of provocation.

A body in all its glorious celebration.

If only I could see the person naked.

Oh what a temptation.

Hardening my new sensation.

Appealing to the eye.

Giving me a physical high.

Humpty

Humpty dumpty sat on the wall. Humpty had a big fall. I have a feeling that will steal the wrath. All hell broke loose on the path. I'm shattered beyond belief. That I'm filled with grief. It's not that I like chicken but beef. I feel physical pain as a brain drain. Out of options I'm overweight. This is my state stop food plate. I can exercise but skate. Lose weight in order to find my mate.

03/21/23

Hope

I don't lose hope for in GOD we trust.

Don't mope for rust.

Good times will come with bread crust.

Say so for you must.

Not everything is lust California or bust.

Nor everything lost for what is the cost.

I pray to GOD in heaven.

The seas will come in seven.

All that is plenty showering like confetti.

There will be a party eating spaghetti.

Hope is not a dope that tethers back and for like a rope.

Or to look into the horoscope nor a mind scope.

Or a problem to cope.

Things will get better not a wet letter.

I don't lose hope nor will I mope.

Horton Plaza

Today I went in a convoy of 7 today to Horton Plaza without my raza.

I spent it eating Indian food that I shared with Rudy.

It was a pleasure to be followed as a leader while I saw a cutey.

We went to Sam Goody where Noelle bought a music C'd.

I enjoyed the music so pretty.

There were many people shopping.

I could just imagine Mary Poppins.

Lilia bought cookies while we ate lunch.

She was following a hunch .

I did not buy anything except food, however it was good.

There were so many stores I could not count the scores.

11/17/09

Hanuka = Chanukah

Agora es Hanuka tyempo de asender las kandelas. =
Now is time for Chanukah to light the candles.

I resitar las berachot en ke yo ambezo tefilot.= And as I
recite the blessings in which I learn the prayers.

Munchas veses tengo sintido al Dio le pido.=
Many times I have heard to G-D I ask.

Muncho de azete para la hanukia.= A lot of oil for the Chunikiah.

Ma yo uzo las kandelas en vez de azete.= But
I use the candles instead of the oil.

Munchos hanukiyot yo merki hanuka alegre para mi.=
Many chanukiot I bought happy chanukah for me.

Mozos los Sefardim estamos dispersos en el galut.= We the
Sephardim are dispersed throughout the diaspora.

Ma ankora vamos asistir una kandelika ceritir.= But now
we are going to assist one little candle to melt.

Bimuelos kon azete vamos kumer djugar kartikas ala sefardiya de
una mujer Senalikliya.= Cinammon Fritters of Matzah with oil we
are going to eat,play cards Sephardic style from a Senalik woman.

Porke Hanuka linda para mi ?= Why happy Chanukah for me?

Munchas kandelas asendimos el korasoniko ya partimos.=
Many candles we light for my little heart we leave.

12/24/19

Halloween

Halloween is a time of spooks.

Time for candy and dandy costumes.

A time of merry making for pizza and soda.

Being with new friends is the time of autumn
and the change of colors on the leaves.

Dark nights chilly to fright like dynamite.

Everything in the mix Dia De Los Muertos Nov1st and second.

I love the plethora of things like mary gold flowers,incense and candles.

Dead Skulls Mexican sweetbread.

The smell tells what the season is all about.

I love trick or treating. That's a Mexican beat.

As time for black and orange.

10/25/19

Hanuka 12/03/20

Ahora este dia de Diciembre encenderemos los dos velas para januka=
Now it is the day of December to light the candles for Chanukah. .

Jugaremos al topo dreidel en que apostamos monedas
de chocolate Hanukkah gelt.= We shall play the dreidel
in which we bet chocolate coins Chanukah gelt.

Dire bendiciones antes de encender las luces en la tarde. = I shall
say the blessings before lighting the lights in the afternoon.

Tocare musica Sefardi de hanukkah en ladino. = I will play
the Sephardic music of Chanukah in JudeoSpanish.

Yo no soy Judío mezquino sin tomar vino.= I am not a
stingy Jew without drinking wine for Chanukah.

Como decimos en ladino todo en tino haci se hace la fiesta rodeados
de familia y amistades.= Like we say in Ladino everything in mind
that's how we celebrate surrounded by friends and family.

Leemos en el sidur para conmemorar estas 8 noches de Januka.=
We read in the siddur to commemorate the 8 nights of Chanukah.

Hasta que se prenden las luces de cada noche y termine
de quemarse no arrodillarse.= Until they light up each
night and finish of burning and not kneel down.

Oiremos cantadoras en ladino que no son me vino los
milagros yo adivino.= We will hear the singers in JudeoSpanish
that they are not wine the miracles I devine.

No es shabat con el pan y el vino.= It is not
the sabbath with bread and wine.

Esto Dios quiso para nuestro destino.= This is
what G-D wanted for our cestiny.

Birmuelos con leche caliente y te.= Birmuelos of matzah
and cinnamon sugar with hot milk and tea.

Me alegra el corazón con mayor razon.= It
gladdens my heart with great reason.

Amor quiero este hanukkah lindo maravillas tengo yo sin vino.=
Love I want this Chanukah beautiful marvels have I without wine.

Soy el único de mi familia que observa esta solemnidad
sin caridad. = I am the only one in my family that
observes that solemnity without charity.

Tomo fotos de las luces sin prender las cruces estrellas de
David se ponen sin vid.= I take pictures of the lights without
turning on the crosses the stars of David are put in the vine.

Ahora cantamos al Dio alabamos.= Now we sing to G-D we praise.

Quiero saber donde esta mi Judia que no viene ni de noche ni de
dia.= I want to know where my Jewess does not come day or night.

Me di por vencido jamás al Dio el Pedido.= I gave
up I never have to G-D the petition.

Que este hanukkah me de mujer sefardita que le digan mijita.= That
this Chanukah he gives me of a Sephardic woman to say my daughter.

Espero mucho este sezon no sea desapercibido sin
razón a todo un corazon.= I wait much this season not
be unperceived without reason with all a heart.

Felices pascuas de hanuka.= Happy greetings of Chanukah.

12/03/20

Happy Birthday Lincoln

It took a Civil War for you to free African American slaves. During your time Mr.President Lincoln North and South fought.

Through war freedom was bought. You did not live long as the they say in the song.As you celebrated at the Opera house you were assassinated. The hunger of the south for vengeance was not abated. The assassin Wilkes Booth was a one legged fugitive. Mr. President from my perspective. You paid with your life. Your woman became a widowed wife. Your time on earth was cut like a knife. But as a matter of fact you were shot in the back. Yet the south was occupied still its a pity you died.They proclaimed emancipation throughout the South.

02/12/21

Hatred Against Minorities

Hate first it was Black and Latino now its Asian and Pacific Islander.Hateful remarks that hate sparks. One form or another is unacceptable. It's Zero tolerance why can't we all get along.

I am Latino and Spanish Jew if I knew what would spew. Sorry Julie, you brought it to my attention. Now I can empathize with you so sorry you were offended. I hope this can be mended.

All my life I have experienced racism directly from caucasians and from people of color. I am a witness to this barbarity. This hate filled depravity. It's so bad it gives me cavities. To God I look for solutions to life's evolution. As a Poet I say it with elocution.

Let's work together for the common good of our nation.

03/20/21

Heureux=Happy

Je suis heureux pour toi.= I know I am happy for you.

Aujourd'hui c'est votre anniversaire=Today your happy birthday.

Joyeux anniversaire.= Happy Birthday.

Tout le monde te souhaite bonne fête.=All the
world wishes you a good celebration.

Félicité,Salut,L'argent.= Happiness,Health, Money.

Je dis la vérité avec mon coure.= I say the truth with my heart.

Vous êtes un cher ami.=You are a dear friend.

Le grace a votre Sante.= The grace to your health.

10/25/2010

I am here

Iam here guided by the hand of GOD. I never thought I would
be here in Malibu. Out of the blue. The VA brought me here I
can't believe as I stare do I dare. It's a place in Montare. It's good
not to be scared of my food and not to tear. Life surprised me
. The place is a peaceful space. Slow is the pace. Therapeutic
my trace. GOD is my ace. I am here with my derriere.

02/04/23

Io Sono Ragazzo = I Am A Young Man

Io sono ragazzo ma non sono pazzo. La vita non sempre è dolcissima. Ma signorina è bellissima. C'era qualcuno al ventuno. Non sono Argentino. Bianco e blu su bandiera. Come L'estera.

Italia e la sua terra. Ancora il signore e uno amatore.= I am a young man but not crazy. The life is not always very sweet. But the miss is very beautiful. It was someone 21. I am not an Argentine. Blue and white flag. like the exterior. Italy is its land. Still the sir is an amateur.

02/04/23

I Have Things To Do

I have things to do to pay my phone. Change that tone.Eat a scone for breakfast.I need to do what's that fool it ain't cool. Find me a tool to go to school. I know my way as they say to come today. I reach for the sun trying to have fun. I see my face with no lace. Watch out for that mace! Only the lonely why are you so bony. Tit for tat and all that. GOOD has my pack not in a sack. Tod got stacked as if he cracked. Nowhere will you grow a pair no my name is not Cher.

02/06/23

Io Vuoi = I want

Dove il mio sogno Americano soltanto DIO saprà la ragione.=Where is my American dream only GOD knows the reason. La verità non è più lontana di là montana.=The truth is not and too far of the mountain yonder. Che sai dove e quando Io sarai ricchi e non poveri.= That I know where and when I will be rich and not poor. Una casa piena di fiori il suspenso me ammazza. = A house full of flowers, suspense kills me. Dietro il cuore Io qualche giorno Io farei ricchi. = Inside the heart I someday I will become rich. Non lasciare una gonna senza l'oro e argento.= Don't leave a skirt without gold and silver.

02/25/23

I Must

I must get stabilized to achieve my objectives. I have arrived at a new conclusion: Independence / Freedom/ New Family. I must go back to get housing..I must go back to college and get a dog.I want and must need a girlfriend. I must work on myself as well as recover. There is much at stake. If only I would let the anger go I must. I must stay stabilized and out of the hospital. I must no longer be a revolving door in the hospital. I must clearly think of the future and how my actions affect me , my family and friends. I must learn to cook, shop, clean and organize my apartment once I get housing. I must go to the University. I must make my dreams come true. I must have faith in myself

03/04/23

Io Penso Che = I Think That

Io penso che la gente mi seguirà in autostrada.= I think
that people will follow me in the highway.

Io sto in citta.= I am in the city.

Mia macchina stai prono accidente. = My car is prone to accidents.

Io credo che tutto il mondo in la lupa.= I think
that everyone is in the magnifying glass.

Io non so chi sono ma stai in camera infraganti.= I don't
know who they are but they are in candid cameras.

L'amica mia me dice non fare cosi.= My friend tells me not to do this.

Voglia di andare lentamente.= She wishes that we go slowly.

Non lavorare così intenso.= Not to work like this intensely.

Andiamo a la corte.= Let's go to the court.

Io prego aiutami Dio! = I pray help me God!

Solo Dio sai come fa.= Only God knows how to do.

02/01/19

Insensível= Insensible

Incredivel muitas coisas insensível.= Incredible many things insensible.

Não sei que achar a DEUS PAI vou chamar.= I don't know
what to think of the GOD the FATHER I will call.

Como me sinto muito mal e como Portugal deixou
Macau.=I feel very bad and like Portugal left Macao.

Insensível eu achei por uns quantos passei.=
Insensible I thought for a few passes.

Minha mãe me perguntou se a cara te ajudo.= My
mom asked me to my face. I help you.

O Coronavírus Covid19 destroçou minha felicidade, agora não tenho saudade.=
The coronavirus covid19 destroyed my happiness,now I don't have nostalgia.

Ninguém sabia o que a China teria que o mundo destruiria.= No
one knew what China had that the world would be destroyed.

Deus vai ficar na China muito mal e diz meu coração.=
GOD is going to China very badly and says my heart.

Lembra todo nesta vida se paga.= Remember you pay for everything in this life.

Castigo de Deus e a praga.= Punishment of GOD and a plague.

Tudo isso foi pra uma ração, um sentimento forte e a emoção.=All
this is for a reason, a feeling strong and an emotion.

Agora estamos pedindo a DEUS perdão e ajuda mais nao
e minha nariz estornuda.= Now we are asking GOD for
forgiveness and help but not and my nose sneezes.

Cobrindo minha cara com máscara e pra que chorar.=
Covering my face with a mask and for what to cry.

Luvas em minhas mãos lavando as então.=Rain
in my hands, washing even though.

Só DEUS sabe o fim isto é tudo pra mim.= Only GOD
knows the end of this and other for me.

05/18/20

I Am Reborn

I am reborn. I am back in my native city. Where the flowers seem so pretty. I got tired of the nitty gritty that was Temecula. San Diego is minha terra nae eu te quero mais.= San Diego is my native land that I love more. Ninguem sabe porque acho que acho na lei esto a minha fei.= Noone knows why I think that think it is the law it's my faith. A revivir mi felicidad sin caridad a San Diego mi lealtad.= To revive my happiness without charity to San Diego my loyalty. Ancora sono felice stare cui in San Diego Dove io voluto andare tutta la vita. Now I am happy to be here in San Diego I want to be there all my life. La cite de San Diego estil bonne chance pour moi pas cue je non dit te toi en chante pourquois.= The city of San Diego is a good chance for me but not I say shut up I am charmed why. La sivdad ande yo nasi es ke yo pasi ainda me ambezi mi ladino kerido para fruchiguarlo.= The city where I was born where I spent it even though I learned my beloved Ladino to multiply. It is my native city where I am from. I am reborn.

Je Suis Joyeux = I Am Happy

Je suis joyeux de belle vue . Une personne de la société est compliquée. Je veux voir ma vie comme un accomplissement sans me lamenter que je ne peux brûler. Jamais je fais dos à dos pour moi est gros. Les choses sont tranquilles dans ma ville.= I am happy with the beautiful view. One person of society that is complicated. I want to see life like an accomplishment without me lamenting that I don't burn. Never I fais dos a dos for me its big. The things are tranquil inside my city.

02/04

Je Suis Contfortable = I Am Comfortable

Je suis confortable avec ma langues etrangere e poesie.= I am comfortable with my foreign languages and poetry. Les choses me donner en pout de paix. =The things give me a bit of peace. J'ai beaucoup de purpose de vie. = I have much of a purpose of life. Je suis contente avec le simplicite' cotidiennne. = I am content with the simplicity of daily life. Il y a le chance pour ameggliore' mon sentire de pensee'. = There is a chance to improve my sense of thinking. Je corresponde a les gens de ville. = I correspond to the city people.

04/11/23

J'oublie= I Forgot

J'oublie beaucoup mon francais!= I forgot most of my French.

Je ne sais écrire bien= I don't know how to write well.

Tu viens d'un pays Anglophone qui préfère parler seulement L'Anglais.= You come from an Anglophone country that prefer only speak English.

N'est pas les autres langues etrangere.=
Not the other foreign languages.

Comment ça va ça va être difficile pour moi parler et écrire au français= How goes it it goes difficult for me to speak and write the French.

N'est pas la habitude.= It is not the custom.

Je désire mieux parler et écrire français.= I desire to better speak and write French.

Me manque la practice.= I lack practice.

Vous pratiquez avec moi.= You practice it with me.

Dit quelque chose.= Say something.

Pour moi les choses sont complexes.= For me the things are complex.

11/18/09

Je Deteste'=I Hate

Je deteste' a le cite' de Temecula a mon jeune seour et votre mari.= I hate the city of Temecula and my sissy and her hubby.

Je laissez beaucoup la maison pour retourner a San Diego ma vie estil fait accomplit.= I leave a lot the house for returning to San Diego but my life is a done accomplishment.

Je dit merci a Dieu que ce ca.= I say thanks to GOD for that.

o la la o la la.

Je suis la petit mort voulez-vous mor comfort.= I am the little death that wants my comfort.

Deja il ya n'est pas Je suis folle une drole parles-moi.= A;ready it is nothing I am crazy one funny speak to me.

Je ne sais quoi.= I don't know.

Un batard le mari de mon jeune soeur me dire frappe' mon ceoure.= A bastard the husband of my sissy hits my heart.

Ke Aremos Mozos ?= What Shall We Do

Mozotros stamos kansos de el kamino.= We're tired of the road. Dinguno sabe orasyonar komo mi nono Albert.= Noone knows how to pray like my grandpa Albert. El kal sefardista en Siatle se yama no lo so.= The Sephardic temple in Seattle I don't know what it's called. Agora vinemos kon la famiya a Gresya i Turkia.= Now we are going with the family to Greece and Turkey. Estos paises mos bivimos e morimos de djoven a aedado de la facha a la mortaja.= In these countries we lived and died from young to old from diaper cloth to burial shroud. Nasimos i morimos en la bida. = We are born and die in life.

03/07/23

Korona = Corona

Munchas famiyas no selaniklis sofrieron muncho en
Estados Unidos.= Many families not Thessalonians
suffered much in the United States.

Adonai save lu ke afito es la postema de korona virus
no un diadema.= GOD knows what happened to
the pimple of CoronaVirus not in a diadem.

Fasta kuando finira la mabula de covid19 por todo el mundo.=
When will we finish the deluge of covid19 for all the world.

Dinguno save fasta ke profundo.= Noone
knows until how profound.

Ayinara leshos ke seyga un kohen o un leyva os kuri.= Evil eye
far from us it will be with a priest or levite to cure us.

Al DIO alto mos prokuri.= To GOD most high find us.

ES tiempo de Simon Bar Yochai en la profondina dela mar ke
todos pyedramos muestro saar.= It's the time of Simon Bar
Yochai in the deep of the sea that we all lose our troubles.

De gota a gota si mueri la djente.= From drop
to drop yes death to the people.

Kualo va afitar di repenti?=What is going to happen?

Ojos di moloch estan pregonando merrekiya vino la
noche se peryo el diya.= Eyes of Moloch looking for
sadness came the night and the day was lost.

Solikos en el mundo fraguamos sin kompaniya andamos.=
Alone in the world we built without company we went.

Hicth nada mos yevimos ni el parnasa kedimos.=
Nothing we took nor the living wage we stayed.

Yoramos muncho vino bevimos el blanko yayin.=
We cried a lot and drank the white wine.

Blanko no mavi es el mayim Resitar taanit i beracha al DIO pedir muncha tefila.= White not blue is the water reciting Taanit and blessings to GOD to ask much prayer.

Ya no puedo komer avramila.= I can't eat plums.

05/18/20

Kasika=Little house

Yo kero mi kasika en Chula Vista morar kon la schejina
i los mezuzot.= I want my little house in Chula Vista to
live with the the holy spirit and the doorposts.

Bendizir ande yo vo kontente kantando las kantigas i romansas.=
Bless where I go happy singing the songs and romances.

Sentir al kantor en el kal komer kezo kashkaval don dolmas i
pishkado de salsa agristada.= Hear the Cantor in the synagogue
eat hard cheese with lettuce wraps and fish with mayonnaise.

Boyos kon chokolata i kave turko.=Sweet rolls
with chocolate and Turkish coffee.

Poder fazer komida Sefardi inkluso el tipishti o los
mogados de almendra.= To be able to make Sephardic
food including tipishti or almond macaroons.

Un pokitiko de myel kon un panesiko.= A
little of honey with a little bread.

Me muero por komer lo muestro en mi mupak.=I
die to eat what is ours in my kitchen.

La delisia ke komemos komo los yaprakes esto para
mi es la kasika.= The delicacy that we eat like the
stuffed grape leaves this is for the little house.

Kon una novia de mi eskojer ke seya Sefardita.= With a
girlfriend of my choosing that she be a Sephardic girl.

Gizar la geyna kon bimbriyo para komer en mi kasika.= To
cook the chicken with quince to eat in my little house.

Agora so felis kon las delisias ansi kero la kasika para mi.= Now I am
happy with the delicacies so I want for my little house for me.

Ke Ago Agora= What Do I Do NOW

Sin Tefila i tora ke ago agora?= Without prayer
and torah what do I do now?

Me siento sin nave en la mar.= I feel like without a ship in the sea.

Komo yaprakes sin paladar.= Like leaves without a palate.

Kero dishir kadish ma no lo puedo meldar.= I
want to say Kadish but I can't read it.

Ay ke kadar la bida vo konsakrar.=There is a
measure of life I will consecrate.

Ande estan mis keridos Sefardim pedridos por la faz del mundo.=
Where are my dear Sephardim lost throughout the world.

Yo kero mi kumida Sefardi.= I want my Sephardic food.

Algen kon ken echar lashon dulse.=Someone
with whom to speak in Ladino.

Kontar kuentos de Djoha.=Count stories of DJoha.

Sentir las romansas i kantigas.=Hear the romance and songs.

Ma agora ay Ladinokomunita una komunidad virtuala por internet.=But
now there is Ladinokomunita a virtual command via internet.

Yo skrivo kon un ladino flako no es el del los aedados ke
se estan muriendo kada anyo.=I write with a weak ladino
it is not of the elders who are dying each year.

Las Cosas = The Things

Las cosas que suceden solo a Dios lo pueden. Las mujeres son como un barco multi colores como el arco. Para mi son difíciles de conseguir especialmente cuando voy a partir. Solo Dios sabe las cosas para no prender esposas. La vida no es color de rosa en pro de mujer acosada ya no tiene esposa. Todo relampaguea igual que una estrella. Las mujeres son peligrosas con un cuerno de chivo que me caigo en el estribo. = Things that happen only GOD can. The women are like a multicolor boat like the rainbow. For me they are difficult to acquire especially when I'm going to leave. Only GOD knows things for not to take wives. Life is not the color of roses in pro of a women accosted I don't have a wife .Every thing is lightning same as a star. The womenare dangerous with a machine gun that falls in the stirrup.

02/04/23

Little Boy

Dear little,

   I wish what happened to you at 7 years had not occured. If you had family or a friend to watch over you would have been protected. It's not your fault it's probably if you had been scared of those two men this would not have happened. GOD only knows what you were going through. You bled from your booty and did not know what was going on. Your father, a Vietnam Vet, would've been killed and he would have been taken away. Again Again GOD intervened because of the schock you blocked out the rape to you. It caused you sexual confusion, poor little one you were all alone when it happened. Only time and therapy will heal your wounds and GOD's love along with your family.Keep your chin up don't give in or give up. GOD bless my dear boy little.

03/03/23

Las Cosas = Things

En el poker usó la As. =In poker I use the ace .Yo me mantengo ocupado todo es como DIOS ha dado.=I keep myself occupied everything is how GOD has given. Busco la dicha con su hado.= I look for luck with its destiny or fate. El tiempo está convencido. Salen de la iglesia el clero.=They come out of church and the clergy. Mucho hay que aprender.= There is much to learn. Tener experiencia es saber.= To have experience is knowledge. A esta Mujer voy a volver.= To this woman I will return. Aun presente es para desaparecer.= Even though at present it is to disappear. De qué me quejo es al espejo.= Of what do I complain to the mirror. Un dedo punto así y dos me despejan por esto se alejan. = One finger point like this and two clear for they go away.

03/15/23

95

La Clase = The Class

Me gusta la clase de nutrición con Anya la Polaca. Ella me enseña mucha saiduria de la comida nutritiva.= She shows me much of the knowledge of nutrition. Es algo muy ligero que yo quiero.=IT is something very light that I love. Ha Sido una experiencia buena para mi.= It has been a good experience for me. Es una luz en mi camino para perder peso. = It is a light in my path to lose weight. Siempre nos sirven té con mucha fe.= She always serves us tea with much faith. Tod tienes su mas y su menos. = Everything has its max and its least . Aún hay que aprender a combinar nutrición con la cocina. =Even though I have to learn to combine nutrition with the kitchen.

04/23/23

Luna

You are loving and caring I'm going to miss you. Especially looking into your caramel eyes. Your black fur, your Zach's fur baby with the white tips of your paws. You like to take off on Zach but you don't talk smack. She is friendly to boot. Ah girl, don't shoot. Luna, you are chien mechant but not a debutante. You make me feel like I am taking straws. You have no dyes in your eyes. Playful as ever girl you take me for a twirl of a baton. You it's you that is fun.

04/27/23

Los Días Soleados = The Sunny Days

Con los días soleados se calienta piel se hace color miel. = With the sunny days the skin gets hot it becomes honey. El bronce que tengo ni blanco ni negro.= The tan I have nor white nor black. Es mas integro.= It is more integrity. Siento calor y huelo el olor de la naturaleza. = I feel the heat and smell nature. Normal no es espesa.= Normal it is not thick. Diamantes o topazio nos calienta el cabello lacio.= Diamonds or topaz it heats up our straight hair. La claridad del día afecta la mente de uno o la gente. Me siento bien en lo caliente con sombra. = I feel good in the hot with shade. Templado no mucho calor en la alfombra.= Temperate not much heat in the rug.

04/27/23

La Pluja = The Rain

La pluja es moltissim o ploure molts.=The rain is much it rains a lot.

Seu molts fred.= It is very cold.

Jo podeu sentir el fred.= I can feel the cold.

El temps mejorar.= The weather will get better.

02/05/19

La Luvya= The Rain

La luvya korri muncho.= The rain runs a lot.

Ke no kero muncho friyo.= That I don't want much cold.

Agora es un diya de friyo.= Now it is a cold day.

La djente va ansina en prisa de skola o lavoro.= People
go like this in a hurry to school or work.

El Dio mos ayudi de todo Saar.= God help us from all trouble.

02/05/19

Le Temps = The weather

Je sentir difficile.= I feel difficult.

La vie est difficile pour moi.=Life is difficult for me.

quand la pluie suivra.= When the rain follows.

Je pense on l'ete.= I think in the summer.

Avec le soleil chaude.= With the hot sun.

Les jours d'été avec les choses chaudes.= The
days of summer with the things hot.

02/05/19

La Lluvia= The Rain

La lluvia ha estado pessima.= The rain has been heavy.

Me he mojado, está lloviendo a cantaros.= I
am wet it is raining cats and dogs.

El sol sale por momentos.= The sun comes out for moments.

Pero desaparece el sol y otra vez la lluvia.= But it
disappears the sun and again the rain.

Bueno todo a prisa.= Well everything in a hurry.

02/05/19

La Cuina= The Kitchen

A cuire les aliments.= To cook the food.

Me donne des aliments molts delicious.=
They give me very delicious food.

Jo soc contente aixi.= I am content like this.

Tot suigi avant total dies de mi vida a casa.= All
follow before all the days of my life to home.

Non podeu despertar aquest moment.= I can't wait for this moment.

Ma ancora jo podeu facer aixi.= But now I can do like this.

02/05/19

La Vita=Life

La vita sorrisi per me.= life smiles for me.

Qualcuna me dai un bacio.=There is one that gives me a kiss.

Un'altra che mi abbraccia.= Another that hugs me.

Nessuna me lascia un morbo che lavorano. = Not
one leaves me a disease that works.

Insieme piano piano vedere un amore forte Yisel pensa in me.=
Together softly softly see a strong love Giselle thinks of me.

Non vuoi lasciare a Sayana.= I don't want to leave Sayana.

Yisel non è morta di fame e una futura moglie.=Gisele
is not dying of hunger she is a future wife.

Creduta non disputa a me.= She believes no does not dispute with me.

Una storia di vita che cresce un amore piano piano
piano piano piano piano forte.=A story of life that grows
a love softly softly softly softly softly strong.

Come un cammello che mangia quella e la mia felicità.
= Like a caramel that eats and is my happiness.

Aspero un bambino di quella dopo il matrimonio di sposare.
= I expect a baby from her after the marriage of husband.

Io vuoi un piccioli varone che farà un uomo.= I want
a baby boy which will be a man someday.

Cominciare una famiglia ella, io ed il bambino.=
Start a family her,I and the baby.

Solo Dio sai la verità fra poco tempo succederà.= Only
God will know the truth in little time it will be.

Io sono stanco come celibato.= I am tired of being a bachelor.

La vita me sorrisi molto.= Life smiles on me.

02/16/20

100

Lord Help

Lord help me find peace through this storm of CoronaVirus. Help me stay healthy from the disease and not transmit it to no one.

Show me the way to redemption by prayer and meditation as well as soul searching for a solution to humanity's problem. God please show me the

way to give me strength to deal and cope with this situation. Please Lord give us an antidote to stop further deaths and contagion. Help us find the way to inner peace.

Deliver us from all this evil my creator for the good of the elders, pregnant women, children and sick people. I I know these are trying moments for the rest of the world not just China.

Show the way to a more serene healthy world lord. I know you will hear my prayer and meditation for this covid-19.

03/16/20

Lune Et Vénus = The Moon And Venus.

La nuit de lune croissante et venus brûler la planète rouge.= The night of the crescent moon and venus burns the planet red.

A droite de la lune.= To the right of the moon.

J'observe dans la nuit non éclairé.= I observe inside the night it's not an eclair.

Pour m'inspirer à regarder les étoiles et la planète Vénus.=I am inspired to look at the stars and the planet Venus.

Je suis content de voir les constellations du ciel bleu.= I am content to see the constellations of the blue sky.

Je me merveille pour une nuit très obscure et non claire estil froid.= I still marvel for a night very obscure and not clear, still cold.

Je peux sentir les sensations dans mon coeur et corps profondément la passion du ciel bleu.=I can feel the sensations in my heart and body profoundly, the passion of the blue sky.

Je suis contente avec la nature, écouter les grilles et les animaux au dehors avec la belle nuit que non briller beaucoup.= I am content with nature, to listen to the crickets and the animals outside with the beautiful night that does not shine much.

Les autres étoiles ne brillent pas la plupart comme la lune et Vénus.= The other stars do not shine like the rest of the moon and Venus.

Je vais dans ma chambre pour le raison de la nuit fraîche et froide.= I go inside my room for the reason of the night, fresh and cold.

Simplement je suis très agreable le ciel bleu qui montre le crescent de la lune et Vénus qui brille beaucoup dans la nuit noire obscure d' hier avril 26, 2020.=Simply I am very agreeable the blue sky that mount the moon and Venus that is shining much in the black obscure night of yesterdays April 26, 2020.

04/26/20

Lumbre= Fire

Lumbre a voces altas con todas las faltas.= Fire in
high pitched voices with all the faults.

La lumbre nada renuevan.= The fire does not renew.

Los bomberos luchan no enhuevan.= The
firefighters battle but don't hatch.

Arduamente luchan de repente. = Hard battle all of a sudden.

La lumbre muy frequente el exodo de la gente.= The
fire frequently the exodus of the people.

Picaso todo esto en mi mente evacuaciones.= Pick
axing everything this is in my mind evacuations.

Brotas todas las emociones.= All the emotions shoot forth.

Tristes son mis canciones.= Sad are my songs.

Esto cambian las relaciones.= This changes the relations.

Lumbre esta en la cumbre.=The fire is in the peak.

Tantos sue~nos perdidos sus due~nos dan latidos.= So
many dreams lost thier owners give throbbing.

Mea culpa,mea culpa sin quien se disculpa.= My
fault,my fault without someone to expulcate.

Para quien se aguanta la lumbre nos ataranta.= For
whom do they endure the fire ties us up.

Unos en la calle con una sola manta.= A few
in the street with only a blanket.

Se duermen en el parque del mate al jaque.=
They sleep in the park check mate.

Jugando ajedrez al reves.= Playing chess backwards.

Vida o muerte cada cual su suerte.=Life or death each his own fate.

Lashon Dulse = Sweet Talk in JudeoSpanish

Lashon Dulse

Lashon dulse del ladino al ladinar.= Sweet Talk of Ladino to wisen.

De mi padre a empadrinar.= From my father to sponsor.

Yo do paras al kashon.= I give money to the drawer.

Por la Keila de Moshon.= By the synagogue of Moses.

Lavoro en tino.= I work in mind.

Kon el buto de preservar i konservar.= With the
aim of preserving and conserving.

Mi erensia del lugar.= My heritage of the place.

L'Espanya i Portugal la lingua avlada trushada no amenguada. =
Spain and Portugal the spoken language brought not diminished.

Ke no kere murir soltanto bivirlo. = That does not want to die but live it.

La Casa De Las Malas Vibras=
The House Of The Bad Vibes

La casa de Manchester Road de Temecula esta espantada.=The house of Manchester Road of Temecula is haunted.

Yo me fui encabronado.=I left like a bat out of hell.

Jamas pense que iva irme para atras a San Diego!=Never did I think I would go back to San Diego!

Ratos muy amargos me hicieron pasar G y el puto.= Very bitter moments they made me pass.

Momentos de depresion muy bruto.= Moments of depression very rough.

Sin tener con que gastar.= Without having with what to spend.

Esto fue malbaratar.= This was to squander.

Todo fue envidia de la gente todo de repente.= Everything was envy of the people all of sudden.

Diciendo que la casa no era mia como tal palo tal astilla.=Saying the house wasn't mine like the chip of the old block.

Nunca pense que iva terminar mal como un podrido tamal.= I didn't think it would end badly like a rotten tamale.

Me quiero ir lejos y jamas verlos al cabron cu~nado y la maldita mana.= I want to go far and never see them again.

Me siento desterrado y amargo.= I feel banished and bitter.

Le Jardin= The Garden

Se passer avec le jardin.=What passes with the garden.

Le jardinière coute que coute tres cher.= The gardener cuts what cuts is very expensive.

Pour e'laguer les palmes.=For prooning the palms.

Je suis displeasire avec l'homme.= I am displeased with the man.

Il me faire fache'.=He makes me angry.

Pour le prix de travail.=For the prize of labor.

Pour moi n'estces pas agreeable et raissonable.=For me it is not agreeable and reasonable.

Tout l'herbes et facile elaguer y compris les arbuste.=All the herbs and are easy to proon and understood the trees.

Mais les Palmes autre chose.=But the palms another thing.

Qu'est ce que ce je ne sais pas.=What is that I don't know anymore.

Seulement des langues Etranger.=Only the foreign Languages.

Pour moi le Jardin estil dificile.=For me the garden is difficult.

N'estce pas facile.= It is not easy.

Je suis triste par les situation.= I am sad because of the situation.

08/29/08

Muncha Ansya i Merrekia =
Much Anxiety and Trouble

Muncha ansy i merrekia kada diya.= Much anxiety and trouble
each day. Yo me desespero i non kero yorar.= I am desperate and
don't want to cry. I dont know when to escape this to improve. Ke
se puede fazer dinguno savi si va floreser. = Who can do and no
one knows if they are going to flourish. Los diyas pasan komo ayre
bolando i mis pachas andando. = The days pass like air fly and my legs
walking. Ken me kere a mi .= Who loves me. Yo non so muyi alegri.
= I am not very hapopy. Soltanto dunke vamos aedados en kismet
. = Only so we go old in fate. A mi me hiere komo konsiguiere = It
wounds me like if I got it. Dinguno es para m .= No one is for me.

02/06/23

Mon Cœur = My Heart

Mon cœur est une fleur. = My heart is a flower. Quis reposer comment
rose'. = Which rests like a rose. Je suis content avec ma tante.= I am
content with my aunt. Je ne pleurais que ce que je fais.La vie n'est pas
facile, le Francais est dificile. = J'aime pour nor tomber.= I love to not
fall. La reflection de mon emotion.= The reflection is my emotion.

02/10/23

Micah

Micah is a tender loving pup. That never gives up. Sweet, loving dog . Who try to guide even in the fog. I got a liking for him without striking Tim. I see This lovable pooch who is not drinking hooch. Easy does it Micah we all love him.

02/17/23

Maintenant Les Choses = Now The Things

J'ai perdu ma connexion avec les choses maintenant. Parce que je cherche la merveille pour faire de bonnes choses.= Because that I look for the marvel to do good things. Dis-moi quelle surprise je repondre.=Tell me what a surprise I answer.

Vous entendre ma vie est compliquée et difficile.= You hear me, my life is complicated and difficult. Maintenant je vois que je suis mise au défi. = Now I see that I am upgrading to a challenge. La vie à une autre voie pour moi pour toujours.= Life to another way for me for everyday. Je veux être heureux.=I want to be happy. Le pourquoi me manque encore. = What I lack again.

02/18/23

Minho Destino = My Destiny

Meu destino é um complexo cheio de inseguridade. = My destiny is complex full of insecurity. Eu estou aterrado por meu futuro não sei quê fazer pra mim?=I am terrorized for my future I don't know what to do for me? Nada mais que Deus me pode ajudar. =Noithing more than GOD can help me. Sentime com incertidumbre.= I will feel uncertain. Que vai fazer de meu destino agora. = What will you be doing of my destino now. Como nós sabemos nossas vidas de repente. = Just like we know our lives all of a sudden. = que foi tudo isso pra mim. =It was all this for me. Que meus cunhados e irmãs me fazem um mal pra mim. = That my brother-in-laws and sisters are going to do evil to me. Só Deus vai saber a verdade. = Only GOD will know the truth.

02/26/23

Mucho= Much

Mucho que quiero yo.= Much I have that I want. Tengo que limitar lo que voy a comprar.=I have to limit what I am going to buy. Ahora no me voy a comer zanahoria.= Now I am not going to eat carrots. Todo no me lo puedo llevar a la gloria.=everything I can't take it with me to Glory. Mis tentaciones con posesiones no hay predicciones.= My temptations with possessions without predictions. Hay sanciones para mis emociones solo gozo en esta vida pero no en la partida.=There are sanctions for my emotions only with joy in this life but not in this parting.

04/03/23

Mar = Sea

Mar cheio d'auga o ceu gris. = The sea is full of water or the gray sky. Os fillos d'as fillas xogando pela auga.= The sons and daughters playing on the waters. Eu ver o canal sedento con areia. = I see the channel thirsty with the sand. Acho praque cale isto as Xornadas. = I think what is this the sojourning. Meu corazon non perdeu a razon.= My heart does not lose its reason.

04/09/23

!Me Encanta! = I like!

Me encanta la poesía y los idiomas extranjeros. = I like poetry and foreign languages. Esos dos pasatiempos son dos de mis meros moles.= These two are my two hobbies which are my jack of all trades and master of some.Pero a mi no me gusta el pozole. = But I don't like pozole. Yo soy hombre de negocios no de los braceros. DIOS me dio estos dones por sufrir mucho aun yo quiero triunfar en la industria disquera y contribuir a las culturas y sociedades del mundo.= G-D gave me these gifts for suffering much even though I want to triumph in the record industry and contribute to the cultures and societies of the world. Esto seria muy profundo.= This would be very profound. Gracias creador tengo consuelo y no duermo en el suelo. = Thanks Creator I have counsel and I don't sleep on the ground. Mis aspiraciones son tan altas que no dejo de so~nar.= My aspirations are so high that I don't stop dreaming. Al propósito yo se que valgo mucho oro de DIOS padre que me protege. = A propo I know that I am worth gold of G-D father that protects me. Yo seguiré hasta que le atine ganar con mi cerebro y muchos mercados internacionales.= I will continue until I hit winning with my brain and many international markets.

04/23/23

Me Dire = Tell Me

Me dire que que de faire la nuit.= Tell me what to do at night.

Toujours librement jamais sans rancune.=
Always freely never out of spite.

Ne pas partir le sentiment contrit.= Not left feeling contrite.

Savoir que que pour se passer de vous dire me que que de faire.=
knowing what to do without you telling me what to do.

Droit au point sans la beaucoup d'agitation.=
Straight to the point without much ado.

Mon ame veut etre eteint avvec cela.= My soul wants to be off with it.

Comme si c'était un équipement.= Like f it was an outfit.

Me prendre aux nouvelles hauteurs.= Take me to new heights.

Je suis sûr que je ne mourrai pas de peur.= I'm sure I won't die of fright.

C'est comme voir avec la nouvelle vue.=It's like seeing with new sight.

Me dire ou je dois aller.= Tell me where I must go.

Sans faisant un show.= Without making a show.

Il fera meme le coup.= It will even the blow.

Alors je dois tracter. = Then I must tow.

Mon corps a sa propre volonté.= My body of its own volition.

Comme si c'était sur une mission.= Like if it was on a mission.

Je ne peux pas traiter l'indecision.= I cannot deal with indecision.

Me dire de former mon esprit.= Tell me to make up my mind.

S'il Vous Plait etre gentil.= Please be kind.

11/27/09

Moitas Vezes = Many Times

Muitas vezes tenho amor com as mulheres.=
Many times I have love with the women.

O amor é difícil demais.= Love is difficult more so.

O coração brota do meu corpo!= The heart shoots from my body!

Lentamente cresci meu amor com a menina que elevou a vista maior.=
Slowly grows my love with the girl that I raise to a higher view.

Não sei como aconteceu. = I don't know how it happens.

Ninguém sabe a razão do que existe.= No One
knows the reason why it exists.

Tudo isso e assim.= All of it is like this.

O amor vem da natureza.= Love comes from nature.

E como existe pra mim.= It 's like it exists for me.

Jan 30th,2019

Many Things Have Changed

Many things have changed. I no longer live in San Diego but Temecula.

I drive but there are no more buses. No longer am
I in a rush or always combing with a brush.

I live with mom at home no longer do I roam. I am
toning down trying to keep from leaving town.

Still I leave home yet I try to do quality time.

I have stability being with my family. However, no sex life or
catching stds strife.More family values living sensibly.

I go to my synagogue and church with my Christian friends. Yes, time
will mend. So many things have changed so I did things to lend.

I am living more humbly without too many expenses.
Seeing things through my lenses. I'm no longer much
of a city dweller or an downtown feller.

I try to adapt to the changes in my life. I want more coming
out of my door. Life throws a wrench in the floor.

01/09/20

Mae=Mother

Voce e minha racao por existir.= You are my reason for existing.

Obrigado a Deus porque me do vida.= I thank G-D for he gave me life.

A existenca de ser e meu parecer.= The
existence of my being i my outlook.

Todo puro vem da minha mae.= Everything
pure comes from my mother.

Ela me quere e nutre de amor. = She loves
me and nutures me with love.

Os lacos maternais ajudam com calor quemte nada mais que iso.=
The maternal ties help with warmth nothing more than this.

A natureza da familha e a forca da vida.= The
nature of family is the force of life.

O amor da mae que da a mim o senso de viver todos
dias da natureza.=The love of a mother that gives
me a sense of living all the days of nature.

Sempre os conselhos dela me dam motivo pra viver un
dia uma noite tal vez.=Always the counsel that is from her
give me motive to live one day one night perhaps.

Pra mim todo iso e natural de andar paso por paso
Avante de vontade boa.= For me everything this is
natural to go step by step forward of good will.

Eu quero moito a minha mae.= I love my mom a lot.

Feliz dia da mae a todos os filhos de mundo.= Happy
day of the mother to all the children of the world.

Obrigado ao Deus por mama e papae que Deus me
dai.=Thanks to G-D for mom and dad that G-d gives.

05/07/20

Memoriale=Memorial

Un giorno di ricordi di te papa.= A day of memories of you dad.

Come se dicesse in tempo corto della morte tua sono quattro anni fa.= How is it sadi in a short time of your death it was four years.

Non c'è di che fare gli cosi ancora che dopo la tua disperazione fu forte emozione per me,Netza,Gaby ei piccioli.= I don't know how to do the things now that after your disappearance it was a strong emotion for me,Netza,Gaby and the kids.

Io sono stanco e manco di te perché dietro io piange perché non stai qui.= I am tired and lacking in you because inside I cry why you are not here.

La vita di un soldato Americano e cittadino morto = Life of a soldier and American citizen dead.

Nessuno sapeva tutto il dolore di mamma che ti stragna molto.=No One knows all the pain of moma that misses you much.

Papa quando vuoi ti sognare ancora e vedeti per la prima volta.= Dad when will I dream your still and see you for the first time.

C qualcuno non sai come fai per andare avanti.= There is one who doesn't know what to do before coming.

Domani Dio saprai che fara sulla me.= Tomorrow GOD will know what to do with me.

Non so se mi sposerò e ai bambini e tu vedrai a me sulla mia moglie.= I don't know if I will marry and have babies and you will come to me with my wife.

Io ho 49 anni, io senza figli e mugghiere non ho la mia propria famigghia.= I have 49 years without children and a wife. I don't have my own family.

Soltanto Una parola che fanno ancora per me illuminare per un sogno.= Only one word I can do still to illuminate me for a dream.

Ciao papa non mi lasci mai.=Goodbye dad don't ever leave me.

05/25/20

Malicia = Malice

La malicia abunda en mil maneras.= Malice
abounds in a thousand ways.

En todos los ambitos de la vida hay cosas como la
pornografia,adulterio,acoso,homosexualidad,drogas,alcohol etc que se
forman las maldades en nuestra sociedad.=In all the ambiances of life
they are things like pornography,adultery,homosexuality,drugs,alcohol
etc that form evil in our society.

Es que el diablo anda suelto en el mundo entero.=
It's that the devil is loose in the entire world.

Para mi esto es en un maleficio las miles formas malignas
combatiendo contra el bien.=For me it is a maleficence
the thousand malignant forms combat the good.

Por ejemplo el aborto es un pecado mortal que es una de
etas miles de manifestaciones.= For example abortion is a
mortal sin that is one of a thousand manifestations.

Pero la malicia sirve un propósito de experimentación para
escoger algo positivo.= But malice serves as a proposal
to experiment for choosing something positive.

Si no experimentamos estos no sabríamos elegir entre
el bien y el mal.=If we don't experiment this we would
not know what to choose between good and evil.

Todo tiene su ying y yang la dualidad de la vida.=Everything
has its yin and yang the duality of life.

Hay muchos casos de malicia igual que bendiciones.=
There are many cases of malice as well as blessings.

No hay que perder estas cosas de la vista en situaciones.=
Let's not lose this point of view in situations.

Quisiera entender el porque de la malicia enteramente.=
I wish I could understand the why of malice entirely

09/05/20

My Dream

I dreamed men in a circle naked.

Waiting for what I don't know.

Crouched,sitting down from a time long gone.

Only mere vibrations and sensations of place unkown.

Steadily I am an empath seeing the scenes unravel.

As if in a tribal ritual of yore.

A fire is blazing.

I can hear drums a beating.

While a shaman dances in a trance commuting with the spirits.

Muntanya=Mountain

Rejection by a uppity white girl.

Introspection tells me wait 2weeks for my reply.

I should have said goodbye.

It was an all time low.

You ho,ho,ho

What makes you think I don't value or love myself.

That I would stoop that low.

Its not up or below.

From now on beyond .

I will wait for a Spanish Jewish girl to give her a twirl.

No matter if I alone in this world.

Better true to me than to you with a haughty view.

You could have said nay or yea.

Yet you dilly dally quite contrary .

Rejection of my desire that was on fire.

Vindictive Bitch you have showed your true colors.

I prefer my solitude than you for you're not my boo.

Move Stale

I wish I could move me and my sister's family.

But we can't because there is no house to go to yet.

I have been waiting for long.

Its the same old song.

To me it seems eternal not changing but choking me.

I have to leave every day so I can cope.

I can't lose hope.

I'm at the end of the rope.

More and more bounded its like if I'm hounded.

Move is stale.

Why won't you bale?

Get out leave me alone its not a subdued tone.

I wait in vain with all the pain.

Waiting for a house to buy like fish fry.

I feel suffocated in a pig sty.

My apartment so small it lacks a hall.

Mezuzah = Parchment Doorpost

Mezuzah

Mezuzah por la puerta.= Doorpost by the door.

Ke abuelta.= That returns.

Terumah

Kitisa

Dishen.= They say.

Ke sosh Djudiyo.= That you are a Jew.

Sefardi atadijo.=Sephardic legation.

Esto fue el kurtijo.= This was the courtyard.

Aman Zeman ponte avlar.= Please put yourself to speak.

Porke yego kartika de Bulgariya.= Because there
came a little letter from Bulgaria.

Para meldar.= To read.

Kuando muncho oskurese.= When much darkens.

Es para Amaneser.= It is to rise of the sun.

Yo meldo mi djurnal kada mes treser.=I read
my periodical each third month.

My New House

I am waiting to see my my new house full of people.

Just like the church and the steeple.

Friends and family gathered about to see my brother-in-law.

Eat and drink.

I think.

Admiring my three story house going up and down.

Like If were a merry go round.

Yet it is on firm ground.

My new house has so much potential.

Awaiting the rain torrential.

It is my muse.

That carries my short fuse.

It is good to know its mine.

For a nice day is fine.

I count my blessings.

I know what I have been missing.

Nor the wear and tare.

I will not stare.

The walls I will not smear.

Living in my new house without fear.

I get a feel for what is there.

From cable, internet and phone.

To talking on the microphone.

Feeling for dialtone.

I need time to rewind.

Provided its kind.

After a while I get tired.

Like drinking coffee and feeling wired.

Waiting for cableman to come.

Like a guitar for me to strum.

Mar=Sea

Solo pienso en el mar de La Jolla.= I only think in the sea of La Jolla. Mirar las focas y gozar de la belleza.= To look at the seals and enjoy the beauty. Sentir que vengo de nobleza.= To feel I come from royalty. Ver los restauranes y tiendas sin sentir las contiendas.= To look at the restaurants and stores without feeling the disputes. Ir con mis amigas y familia a una merienda.= Go with my friends and family to a picnic. Comer birmuelos con membrio para tomarme algo frio.= To eat sweet patties with quince to drink something cold. Sentir la briza del mar jugar un juego de azahar.= Feel the breeze of the sea, play a game of orange blossoms. Oir la musica flamenca.= Listen to the flamenco music. Despues comer las pencas del nopal.= Later eat the fleshy leaves of the cactus. Con rajas de aceitunal y una dafina.= With slices of a olive field and a dafina. Disrutar la agua fresca sin nadar.= To enjoy the fresh water without swimming.

My Day In The Sun

My day in the sun has to come to get my recognition mum. I am a cool cat always going to bat. Will I ever see the day for my deeds without speeds. Always working behind the scenes never being part of the spotlight. I wish it was me that was out of sight in the spotlight. I hunger for respect like I'm on a treck. I die in the shadows always fighting my battles. Who can I turn to? GOD,people,who? I don't have a clue do you? The struggle continues for the lime light therefore I continue to fight. Mayday in the sun will It ever come?

Ma Vie= My Life

Ma vie nestpas joyeaux,quelle que fois folle beaucoup.=
My life is not joyous that once very crazy.

Je parlez mieux que vous de cette chose qui negre.= I
speak better than you of this thing which is black.

Maintenant ou e ma vie douce?=Now where is my sweet life?

Je pleurer tres pitie', malgre' le situation presente'.=I
cry very pitiful,despite the present situation.

Je voulez que changer de mal au bon chance.= I
wish that it changes from bad to good luck.

Ou e mon ceour que chante' liberte',liberte',liberte'
a Dieu a le monde?= Where is my heart that says
liberty,liberty,liberty to GOD and the world?

Ma vie tres dur non facil pour moi!=My life is very hard not easy for me!

Allon a la synagogue pour prier a Dieu pour refua schleima.=Go
to the synagogue to pray to GOD for a healing.

Je suis un Juif.= I am a Jew.

Munchas Bueltas= Many Turns

Munchas bueltas da la bida.=Many turns that life gives.

Ainda no se lo ke topare en este mundo =Even though
I don't know what I will find in this world.

Patron del mundo ayde ayde ayudarre!= Master
of the world hurry hurry help me!

Ande esta la chochma para dizir tora?=Where
is the wisdom to say Torah?

Porke no baylo la hora?= Why I don't dance the Hora?

Los tanyedores no son mis djenitores ansi vyenen los dolores.=
The musicians are not my parents so come the pains.

Algo preto se kale muncho respeto.= Something
black that is necessary much respect.

Kero ambezar lo dulse de la bida.= I want to learn the sweetness of life.

Aki no se kome las proidas.= Here we don't eat the the clams.

Solo kumida kascher tenemos el dover.=Only
Kosher food we have the duty.

Kijera vijitar el kal sefardi en la Turkia =I would like
to visit the Sephardic synagogue in Turkey.

Estambol es una maraviya!=Istanbul is a marvel!

Esto es lo ke kalia.= This is what must be.

Munchas bueltas de bivir un dia.=Many turns of living one day.

Mora=She Lives

Ela mora em Point Loma.= She lives in Point Loma.

Aqui esta a comunidade Luso-Brasiliera pra dancar na capoeira. e cantar um fado.=Here is the Portugese-Brazilian community to dance Capoeira and sing a Fado.

Brasil filha do Portugal nao estamos em funchal.=Brazil daughter of Portugal we are not in Funchal.

Tambem esta os Acores da ilhas incluindo Madeiras.=Also are the Azores Islands including Madeiras.

Eu Lembro o vinho do Oporto.= I remember the wine of Oporto.

Tradicoes e costumes que venha a linguica e chourico pra comer.= Traditions and customs that we have linguica and chourico= sausages for eating.

Com un bolinho doce entremesa de goiabada com queijo.= With a sweet roll a dessert of guava paste with cheese.

Muito tempo que nao vejo.=Long time I do not see.

My Dream

I dreamed men in a circle naked.

Waiting for what I don't know.

Crouched,sitting down from a time long gone.

Only mere vibrations and sensations of place unkown.

Steadily I am an empath seeing the scenes unravel.

As if in a tribal ritual of yore.

A fire is blazing.

I can hear drums a beating.

While a shaman dances in a trance commuting with the spirits.

Muntanya=Mountain

Jo vaig arriva una muntanya.= I go on top of the mountain.

Molts difficil anar hi pedras com un home perdut.=
Very difficult to walk on rocks like a lost man.

I un juich errany que baixa despaci san tancat.= And a
errant jew that goes down slowly w thout closed.

L'entrada de la muntanya.= The entrance of the mountain.

Plora meu cor ploro molts moltissim anys.=My
heart cries it cries many years.

Mar=Sea

Solo pienso en el mar de La Jolla.= I only think in the sea of La Jolla.
Mirar las focas y gozar de la belleza.= To look at the seals and enjoy
the beauty. Sentir que vengo de nobleza.= To feel I come from royalty.
Ver los restauranes y tiendas sin sentir las contiendas.= To look at
the restaurants and stores without feeling the disputes. Ir con mis
amigas y familia a una merienda.= Go with my friends and family to
a picnic. Comer birmuelos con membrio para tomarme algo frio.=
To eat sweet patties with quince to crink something cold. Sentir la
briza del mar jugar un juego de azahar.= Feel the breeze of the sea,
play a game of orange blossoms. Oir la musica flamenca.= Listen to
the flamenco music. Despues comer las pencas del nopal.= Later
eat the fleshy leaves of the cactus. Con rajas de aceitunal y una
dafina.= With slices of a olive field and a dafina. Disrutar la agua
fresca sin nadar.= To enjoy the fresh water without swimming.

My Day In The Sun

My day in the sun has to come to get my recognition mum. I am a cool cat always going to bat. Will I ever see the day for my deeds without speeds. Always working behind the scenes never being part of the spotlight. I wish it was me that was out of sight in the spotlight. I hunger for respect like I'm on a treck. I die in the shadows always fighting my battles. Who can I turn to? GOD,people,who? I don't have a clue do you? The struggle continues for the lime light therefore I continue to fight. Mayday in the sun will It ever come?

Munchas Kosikas= Many Little Things

Munchas kosikas an pasado no todo de mi agrado.=Many things have passed not of my pleasing.

A veses me siento pezgado komo la muerte de mi nona.= At times I feel heavy like the death of my grandmother.

Ke en gan eden kede su persona.= That in paradise may her person remain.

Esto asperando ke me deshen konduzir oto el estado de California.=I am waiting for them to let me drive the car the state of California.

Ansi poder ver la gloria.= So to see the glory.

Agora ambezar komo meldar el livriko de Drivers Ed.

Para dospues skrivir la prova del konduzir.= For later to write the test of driving.

Ansi me puedo inchir el permiso para konduzir.= So that I can fill the permit to drive.

Esto lishiando la ropa para ke este limpia.=I am washing the clothes so it will be clean.

Muchas Veces= Many Times

Muchas veces yo no paso con creces.= Many times I don't pass lavishly.

Se me va y pierde la mente.= It leaves me and lose the mind.

Todo en un dia como torbellino.= Everything in one day like a whirlwind.

Siempre me da mal espino.= It always gives me a bad feeling.

No se que hacer con mis padres = I don't
know what to do with my parents.

Siempre mentadas de madre.= Always cuss words.

Porque no tengo novia y casi puros amgos.= Because I
don't have a girlfriend and mostly male friends.

No se como conocer a las muchachas.= I
don't know how to meet the girls.

Tampoco se me quita la mala racha.= Niether does the bad luck rub off.

Porque la vida me es dura?= Why is life hard for me?

Como si me tortura.= Like if it tortures me.

Yo tengo mi angustia a mi no se me quita.=
I have anxiety it doesn't go away.

Nossos Dias = Our Days

Nossos dias são como um abraco de laço. Ninguém sabe o que
eu vou levar do céu ao paraíso. Sim você ajuda meu Deus. Passo
por passo eu vou seguindo assim pra mim. Sinto minha alma voar
pelo tempo em busca de flores. Tudo isso meus ardores. Deixa isto
que não existo. Nossos dias um dia a vez. = Our days are like an
embrace with ties. Noone knows what will take the sky to paradise.
Without your help my GOD. Step by step I will follow it like that for
me. I feel my soul fly through time in search of flowers. All are my
ardors. Leave these that do not exist. Our day one day at a time.

02/05/23

No Soy Pervertido = Im No Pervert

He visto la figura humana desnuda. = I have seen the naked human figure. Como un punto de vista de no echar la leche de paja.= From a point of view it 's not to choke the chicken. Yo no puedo ser un gilipollas. = I can't be an asshole. Hay que ser honesto el cuerpo humano natural es hermoso. = Let's be honest, the human body is naturally beautiful. Tanto una mujer desnuda o un hombre desnudo son lindos de mirar como Adan y Eva. = Not only a naked woman or man, they look pretty to look like Adam and Eve.Hay mil maneras de usar las Bellas Artes para expresar el cuerpo humano desnudo. = There are thousands of ways to use the Fine Arts to express the naked human body. Está la pintura, la escultura, cerámica, canto, dibujo y finalmente la poesía. = There is painting,sculpture,ceramics, song , drawing and finally poetry. Para mi el cuerpo desnudo es una maravilla. = For me the naked body is a marvelous wonder.

03/03/23

Navidad = Christmas

No hay que hacer nada de convencer = There is nothing to convince.

Solo gente visitar sin actividades mi paladar. = Only
people visit without activities to my palate.

Haciendo nada sin cansar.= Without doing nothing without resting.

Viendo decoraciones con navide~nas canciones .=
Looking at the decorations with Christmas songs.

Tiempo de familias y amistades tiempos de realidades.=
Time for families and friends times for realities.

Comiendo, cantando, visitando y platicando.=
Eating, singing, visiting and talking.

Momentos de espacio caminando un tiempo lacio.=
Moments of space walking a time straight.

Viviendo un dia ala vez sin pescar un pez.= Living
one day at a time without catching a fish.

Navidad con Janucá en tiempos reales sin encender con pedernales.=
Christmas with Hanukkah in royal times without lighting with flints.

Momentos lentos de un espacio sin ceder el ocasio.= Slow
moments of space without giving the occasion.

Es un regalo sin topacio.= It is a gift without topaz.

Todo intenso que yo recompenso.= Everything
intense that I recompense.

Sigo solo y no acompa~nado cada quien por su lado.= I
keep alone and not accompanied each goes their way.

Mucho tiempo reposado Navidad un dia alumbrado.=
Much time restful Christmas a day of lighting

12/24/19

New Beginnings

New Beginnings. No more procrastination!

Putting things off is a sin against GOD!

It's time to clear the air let bygones be bygones.

I feel the renewal of my soul at the esnoga with the
chacham so to at church with my Christian friends.
A time to plan a new not taming shrew.

God has plans for me this 2020 from one to the many . It's
time for my future. Without using a doctor's suture.

I approach the new year without reproach.
The house is clean, not even a roach.

I go about in my car, not a stagecoach. I'm looking
for my silver lining for my new horizon.

I am hopeful with a new beginning with a seventh
inning. Whatever the new year may bring.

01/05/20

Nueva Barrera = New Barrier

Las metas que tengo en mente vienen con barreras.=
The plans that I have come with barriers.

Aun si lo supieras decente.= Even though you knew it was decent.

Todo o nada es de doble espada.= All or nothing is a double sword.

Solo ciertas cosas me agradan. = Only certain things please me.

La poesía a mi no me enfadan.= Poetry does not bore me.

Vivo un día a la vez sin mucho revez.= I live
one day at a time without reversals.

Algo es mejor que nada.= Something is better than nothing.

Escribo mis poemas de pura chiripada.= I wrote my poems of pure luck.

La etapa de mi vida no es la que despida.= The period of my life is not a farewell.

Mis inspiraciones son las fuentes de escribir.= My
inspirations are fountains of writing.

Ahora tengo otro estilo de vivir.= Now I have another style of living.

Te diré la verdad, no puedo mentir.= I will tell you the truth, I can't lie.

Vivo en unas peque~nas ciudades ya ro San Diego pero
existo.= I live in small cities now not San Diego but I exist.

Todo puede ser tengo mis sentimientos mixtos.=
Everything can be but I have my mixed feelings.

La mana de mi alma ámbar a Dios tengo que agradar.= The
heavenly food of my soul is ambrosia to G-D I must please.

Cuando voy a la sinagoga o iglesia con mis amistades
veo las espiritualidades.= When I go to the synagogue or
the church with my friends I see the spiritualities.

Nueva Barrera es revivir mi existencia sin permanencia.= The
new barrier is to revive my existence without permanence.

Todo a mediados de la paciencia.= Everything with patience.

01/21/20

Nuevo A~no = New Year 2021

Estaba dormido con mucho cansancio.= I
was asleep with much tiredness.

Es como todo se veia oscurecido y el dia estaba vencido.= It's like
everything was being seen in darkness and the day was conquered.

Al 2020 es que yo despido.= To 2020 I bid farewell.

Ni musica al oido.= Nor music to my ears.

Todo en la casa era humilde.= Everything in the house was humble.

No bueno que ya no tenemos a Matilde.= Not
good because we don't have Matilda.

Lo recibi al 2021 casi dormido.= I recieved 2021 almost asleep.

Pero yo estoy listo para ver lo que el a~no nuevo 2021 me prepara
para seguir adelante con mi vida.= But I am ready to see what the
New Year 20221 prepares for me to continue forward with my life.

Yo se que Dios tiene un destino bueno para mi.= I
know that God has a good destiny for me.

Con la ayuda voy a comprar casa y retomar mi licencia de conducir.=
With help I am going to buy a house and reacquire my driver's license.

Noche De Embruneser = Night of Darkness

Diya tadre empesa la noche de embruneser.= The
day afternoon starts to darken the night.

La noche es djoven ma eskuresi andando yo i mi madre.= The
night is young but it is obscuring walking me and my mother.

De San Diego a Temecula el viaje toma su direksyon.= From
San Diego to Temecula the trip takes its direction.

Ti~nevlas es la nochada buena al yegar a kaze.=
Hell is the night good to reach the house.

Todo termina ansi de un luguar a e otro luguar.=
Everything finishes like from place to place.

Me paso andando el tyempo en oto kon mi madre para pasarla.= I
spend my time in an auto with my mom to pass the time away.

YO veygo los arvoles, muntanyas montes, yervas penias i flores por
el kaminu ma son sombras.= I see the trees. mountains, mounts,
herbs stones and flowers by the road but they are shadows.

Kon mis pachas adyentro la araba empesan a
da~nar porke so boyli.= With my legs inside the car
they start to damage because I am short.

YO me do kuento de mis sensios de kada i kada koza.= I
get wind of my sensations from each and each thing.

Para mi es desperto del viaje en la noche.= For me
its an awakening of the trip in the night.

Inmientris yo miro los karus en la karrera kon prestes.= In the
mean while I see the cars in the highway with lightening speed.

Ma el jandarma los afera para dar multas.= But
the police is out to give them fines.

Mi madri agyara sin la prestes i la pasimos sin muzika
en el radyo.= My mom arrives without the speed
and we spend it without music in the radio.

Vido nochada empesari ayegimos a kaza yo i mi madre a durmir.= I see the night starting to arrive home I and mother to go to sleep.

Iskapa la iskureser ma yo durmo akedado.= It escapes the darkening but I sleep stationary.

02/08/21

New Year

The New Year is already here.

I look forward to many things.

New house and friends to make.

So many new things to look forward to.

I can see the transformations taking place.

I hope people will remember all the good times spent together.

Opportunity knocks on the door.

Take me with the New Year.

New vistas and horizons before me.

The mountains and valleys of Temecula and Murrieta call.

An hours drive from San Diego.

Novo Incontro=New Encounter

Vou pra mi cidade natal eu nao sou Cabral.=I
go to my native city I am not Cabral.

Meus olhos querem olhar todo que e San Diego Naval.=
My eyes want to see all that is Naval San Diego.

Eu sempre acho em nesta cidade.= I always think in this city.

Aqui eu tenho liberdade.= Here I have liberty.

Sentia muita saudade.= I felt much longing.

Porque eu morava em Temecula.= Because I lived in Temecula.

Nao tem que estar ali.= I don't have to be there.

Gosto lembrar como eu voltar.= I like to remember how I would return.

Todo bem e optimo.=Everything good and great.

Espero todo vai fazer bom como um sonho de som.=I
await all will be good like a dream of sound

O Dia = The Day

O dia e bo que inche do meu corazon.The day is good that fills my heart. Eu sintome mixior as flores non son brancas mais que atoparon moradas.= I feel better the flowers are not white but they're found purple.Gustariame o sol en o dia.= I like the sun in the day. Ceibe estamos en Galiza primeiro grazas a Deus.= We are free in Galicia first thanks be to G-D. Os dias do sol vai chegando co Verao.=The days of the sun are coming with the summer. E un pracer ver a chegada do sol calente xenial.= It is a pleasure to se the coming of the hot sun its great. Deixa que o calor do dia abrace seu corpo. = leave that the hot of the day embrace your body. Meu anversario vo ao viaxe coa sol hoxe. = My birthday I go to the trip with the sun today. = Estou moi ocupado co traballo fixechei sair ao sol.= I am very occupied with work I made to go outside to the sun. Eu fas onte brocear co o sol.= I do yesterday with taking a tan of the sun. Eu vei o sol calente.= I have seen the hot sun

03/25/23

O Ploaie=The Rain

Ploaie o nenorocire nu vine niciodată singură=
Rain never runs out it pours.

Zi ploaie el termina f.= The rainy day is over.

Eu fericit.= I'm happy.

Eu fericit vreme de la be terminat.= I am happy
the rainy weather is almost over.

02.05/19

Ode To Loren Wilson

Ode to Loren you were a friend indeed.

Now we lay you to rest in a heavenly nest.

Amen and he is your vet brother.

God sees you were a father to me amen.

You were there for me in time of trouble,when I couldn't sleep.

You would come and say listen Linda listen. You
would comfort me and keep me company.

For this I remember you and honor your memory even
though Julie and I cry. God Bless your soul. Amen.

01/31/21

On Fire

Four years ago it seems it always happens in October.

Cedar Fire in San Diego County.

Are we going to lose the bounty.

Harris ,Deerhorn new fires this October 2007.

Say prayers to heaven.

What happened October 2003?

I don't want it to be!

Fire started in Malibu,Los Angeles county almost today.

Flames up the wazoo no way.

I hope the place I wanted later won't be haunted.

Fire fire hot on the wire.

The consequences dire.

Will we see no end.

for the fires to mend.

More and more prayer for us to GOD to send.

The smoke ,gray, choke.

Homes burned and people broke.

FEMA called of the hook.

Fire started in Fallbrook.

San Diego sunny hunted down like a bunny.

Governor asked Uncle Sam for money.

Visions opened without Lani.

Fire spreading to our coast.

There is nothing to boast.

No champagne toast.

Human victims roast.

Ocean

I am in water gliding up and down the bay.

Sun shining on the drops from the jungle leaves.

With dew of exotic fruits spreads its aroma.

Pungent fragrance back to the bay to the Ocean.

Spreading its airs to the four corners.

Back and forth with bluish mirth helps me dream.

Oportunidad=Opportunity

Yo tome la oportunidad de conocer a una mujer.= I
took the opportunity to get to know a woman.

No me arrepiento de parecer.= I don't regret to my liking.

El Dios de mis padres reconocer.= GOD of my fathers recognizes.

Me contesto mi peticion cuando yo hice oracion.=
He answered my petition when I did prayer.

Todo se puede para el Todopoderoso.=
Everything is possible for the Allmighty.

Esto se me concedio sin ser lechoso.= This was
granted to me without being lecherous.

Gracias infinitas a la vida.= Infinite thanks to life.

Ahora tendre mi querida.= Now I will have my beloved.

Prichipiko = Principality

En el princhipato de Monako vive el princhipiko kon su padre el rey i famiya la dinastiya Grimaldi. = In the principality of Monaco lives the little prince with his father and family the Grimaldi dynasty. Dinguno aspera ke Frankia tomi Kontrol du su reyno. = No one waits for France to take control of his kingdom. El DIO agora la djente dizi ke va ser de sus pekenyiko pais de edifisyos grandes i el kasino de Monte Carlo. = G-D now and the people say what will be of their tiny country of big buildings and the Casino of Monte Carlo. La djente esta yena atslaha kon paras i korporasyones i sus ombre de komercho. Tyene plaj famosa ande las mujeres se topan nudas ariva los pechos.= It has a famous beach where the women bare their breasts. Ansi son los echos. = that's how business is. Mui lokos atavanados se topan los ombres por ver a las mujerikas de sus keridos. = Crazy to the ceiling the men are looking at the young women of their loved ones. Es komo Venesya o si dizi Veneto ma kon los kanales ansi mezmo komo la sochieta Venezyana.= It's like Venice or it's called Veneto but with the canals and just like the Venetian Society. Se avla Munegasku el diyialekto de Monako.= Monegasque is the dialect of Monaco which is spoken. La sivdad es syete kilometros esta aryento las muntanyas. = It is seven kilometers inside the mountains. Se avla Ingles,i el Franses i el Munegasku son linguas ko ofisyalas. = English, French and Monegasque are co-official languages spoken. La sivdades enternasyolano djente estranyera de todo el mundo viajian ayi. = The international cities and foreign people from all over the world travel there. Munchas vezes e kerido star ayi solo el DIO lo puede fazer realita.= Many times I have wanted to be there and only G-D can make it reality.

04/07/07/23

Pedras Verdes= Green Rocks

Pedras verdes na praia com água fluir.= Green
rocks at the beach with water flowing.

Mantem-me ir.= It keeps me going.

Tao natural e sereno.= So natural and serene.

Especialmente quando está limpo.= Especially when it 's clean.

O oceano próximo as pedras tão verdes.=The
ocean near the rocks is so green.

Pergunta-se para meu e auto-estima.= It
does wonders for my self esteem.

Dar-lhe a cor verde das docas.=Giving it the green color of the docks.

Lembro-me de ir a passeios.= I remember going there for walks.

Lembro-me dever estas pedras coloridas por natureza.=I remember
seeing these beautiful colored stones colored by nature.

Gozo a paisagem que é uma caracteristica.= I
enjoy the scenery which is a feature.

Estas pedras verdes que eu não ouso pisam para este escarregadio.=
These green rocks that I dare not step on for it to be slippery.

Isto é como evito corrida em miséria.=This is
how I avoid running into misery.

Se ao menos o descanso do mundo estava em paz.=
If only the rest of the world were in peace.

Então meus problemas cessariam.= If only my troubles would cease.

Com pedras verdes eu estou contente.= With green rocks I am content.

Isto é o que a terra queria dizer.= This is what the earth was meant.

Posso ficar perdido no mar de verde.= I could get lost in a sea of green.

Tao brilhante,saudável e agudo.= So bright,healthy and keen.

11/19/09

Purim

Time for Plays by the kids. Costumes galore
with ears of Haman on the floor.

A party with Megilat Ester now we say hi at the Schul yes it's no bull.

I look forward to being at other schuls. Support events
in my local Jewish community I approve of.

To be more accomodating without dissipating in Murrieta or
Temecula. Visit congregations to boot sharing in the purim loot.

As many sweets come Purim Lanu Pesaj en la Manu. I know sweets
and candy is what we have a lot of eating without the gab.

Queen Ester and Mordecai are always on my mind
jewish essence is my kind.G-D was invisible all this
time a holocaust was prevented just this time.

But the inquisition and Nazi onslaught was not
avoided yet Purim lives in my imagination.

02/16/20

Pere=Father

Mon père je te regarder avec le ciméterie pour le jour pour le jour memoriale allons y avec ma mere pour donner le fleur rouge gladiolas et fleur blanche de fiancée.=Dad I see you with the cemetery for the day of Memorial day we go with mom to give you flowers red gladiolas and white flower of girlfriend.

Beaucoup de personnes ont visité le cimetière sans lès vase avec de l'es vase avec de l'eau couleur verte.= There are many persons who visit the cemetery without the vase with the water color green.

Je suis joyeux avec maman pour visiter votre place.= I am happy for my mom to visit your place.

Beaucoup de voitures et de personnes pour le salon à votre mort.= There are many cars and persons for the salon to your death.

Dieu les plaisir et vous recibe les choses de moi et ma mere une bannière et fleur.=God is pleased and you receive the things from me and mother with a flag and a flower.

Je me sens bien de coeur et corps visiter à toi.= I feel good of heart and body to visit you.

Je suis contente de faire les choses obligatoire le fidele de fils.= I am content to do the things obligatory of loyal sons.

Je crois que faire une visite est belle.= I think to do a visit is beautiful.

Maman et moi sommes heureux de bonheur pour raconter la vie d'un soldat père, mari et grand-père.= Mom and I are very happy to be able to tell the story of goodwill for the life of a soldier, dad,husband and grandfather.

Nous suivrons les saisons de la vie.= We follow the seasons of life.

05/25/20

Pesaj=Passover

Pesaj en la mano.=Passover in the hand.

El tiempo de limpiar la casa del pan y trigo.= The
time to clean the house of bread and wheat.

Se puede comer mucha carne de res,gallina,pavo,y cordero.=
You can eat much meat, beef,chicken, turkey and mutton.

No mas que no se puede comer levadura Matza se come
varios dias y marachinos de coco con vainilla o chocolate.=
You can't eat leaven Matzah is eat various days and
macaroons of coconut with vanilla or chocolate.

Mucha verdura y fruta se consume y vino o jugo de uva se toma
o agua mineral.= Much green vegetables and fruit is consumed
and wine or juice of grape is drunk or mineral water.

Que no se nos olvide la Hagada y el seder al bajar el sol.= That the the
Hagada and seder is not forgotten in the coming down of the sun.

Con canciones y musica se celebra el pesaj.= With
songs and music passover is celebrated.

Muchas bendiciones se dicen y se comen ciertas cosas simbolicas.=
Many blessings are said and certain symbolic things are eaten.

Gefilte Fish y brisket se come ala Ashkenazia o Migina
shakshuka ala Sefaradia.= Gefilte fish and brisket is eaten
Ashkenazi style or Migina or shashuka Sephardic Style.

Se lee en Yidish, Ladino o Hebreo o Ingles.= Yiddish
,Ladino or Hebrew or English is read.

Ahora estamos atentos con la sinagoga y la congregacion.=
Now we are in tune with the synagogue and congregation.

El rabi pone un vaso de vino.=The rabbi puts a glass of wine.

03/20/21

Qualidades = Qualities

Eu sou bom, terno de bom coração.= I am good , of tender good heart. Aberto amável e incrível como um poeta.= Open,friendly and incredible like a poet. Minhas qualidades são boas em frente a gente.= My qualities are good in front of people.

Estou namorando mulheres que são belezas.= I am falling in love with beautiful women. Tenho atracao persoas inteligentes.=I attract intelligent persons. Ninguém me entende mais.= No one understands more. São poucas pessoas que me conhecem moito bem.= There are few persons that I got to know very well. Ter porquinhos amizxades.=I have few friendships. Quero ter mais amigos e amigas.=I want to have more friends. Mais na persoa não é sempre natural comigo.=But the person is not always natural with me. Estão um pouco.= Is a little. Bizarro e alinhado comigo. = It is bizarre and aligned with me. Espero conhecer melhor gente.= I hope to meet better people.

02/17/23

Quante Cose? = How Many Things?

La cosa buona e chi suona al tempo.= The good thing and it sounds to time. Io fai per dietro = I do inside. Soltanto una parola andò a finire.=Only one word and I come to finish. Le cose faremo una bella strada.= The things we will make one beautiful street. Nessuno sai che io fare così molto vero di te.= No one knows that I do this much truth of yours. Andiamo al mercato per marcare un piatto.= Lets go to the market to buy a plate.

02/18/23

Que Hago ?= What Should I Do?

que Hago con mi vida o mi cuerpo. = What should I do with my
life or body. Yo estoy en el punto de encuentro bien o mal tal
para cual.= I am at the crossroads good or so it is. En cuanto
yo voy haciendo estoy entendiendo.= As I am doing I am
understanding. El colegio, la universidad son buenos no una
fatalidad. =The college,university are good, not a fatality. ?¿Qué
hago en el lago? =What do I do in the lake? Yo tengo mis estragos
sin muchos tragos. = I have my struggles without drinks.

Soy uno que lucha ponte trucha.= I am someone who fights
for attention. Haci es mi perfil como Gil.= My profile is like Gil.
Muchos triunfos por ganar así voy a estar. = Many triumphs
that I win, that 's how I will be. Yo se que puedo conseguirlo
sin decírmelo. = I know I can get it without saying it to me.

03/07/23

Quesería De Mí ?= What Will Be Of Me?

?Quesera de mi ya no se mi camino solo DIOS mediante?=What
will of me I don't know my way only GOD's will? Hay que echar
p'alante.= Let's move forward. Poquitico de Aragonés que es
Charrar Lingua.= A bit of Aragonese that is to speak the language.
Es como andar en una yegua.=It's like riding a mare. Traumatizado,
despelucado no se que decir.= Traumatised, dishevelled I don't
know what to say. Mi familia me rechazó sin prescindir.= My family
rejected me without replacement. Es una pesadilla de la cual no
me puedo despertar ni es maravilla para cortar. =It is a nightmare
from which I cannot awaken nor is it a marvel to give account.
Alejarme alejo corretear como un conejo.= To distance I go far to
run like a rabbit. Siento el despecho hasta mi techo.= I feel the
spite up to the roof. No sé si pueda perdonar allí en el altar.=I don't
know if I can forgive at the altar. Amargo me voy largo.= Bitter I
get lost. ?Quesera de mi soy loco como Dali.= What shall be of

my crazy like Dali. Quiero mejorar mas tengo que escapar.=I want to improve more than I want to escape.? Que Sera de mi cuando madre ya no estes?=What will be of me mother when you are not there? ?Quesera de mi al reves?= What will be of me backwards?

03/20/23

Quando Lascio= When I Leave

Quando lascio al mio amore.= When I leave my love.

Per tanto a la signorina.= For much to the young miss.

Carina che aspetto tutti giorni ed notti.= Dear
that waits all the days and nights.

Dove stai quella belina?= Where is this beauty?

In isole fillipini.= In the Phillipine Islands.

Io la baciare sul abracciare quando arrivare a San Diego.= I
will kiss her and hug her when she arrives in San Diego.

Fare l'amore tutta la notte.= Make love all night.

Quero O Sol= I Want The Sun

Quero beijar o sol do dia.=I want to kiss the sun by dia.

Es que quer resplandeza.= It is that I want resplendedness.

As palmeiras Quattro som.= The palms are four.

Pra mim nao bom.= For me it is not good.

Todo que sao as plantas.= Everything that is plants.

As ervas esta bem.=The herbs are good.

Mais nas palmeiras e mau.= But the palmtrees are bad.

Nao se pode trabalhar.=It cant work.

Todo esto eu lembrar.=Everything is for me to remember.

As palmeiras custan 300 dolares.=The palmtrees cost 300 dollars.

Por podar as folhas de palma.= To proon the leaves of palm.

Nisto me tira a calma.= Those make my calm go away.

O jardineiro mi diz que bom que nao e raiz.=The
gardener tells me how good its not a root.

Quero o sol mais que a lua.=I like the sun more than the moon.

Brilhante como diamante.=Bright like a diamond.

Mentira o jardim que esta bom.= It's a lie the garden is good.

Todo muito caro somo o som.= Everything
very expensive like the sound.

Na grita que saia do meu coracao.= The cry that comes out of my heart.

Nao se vai ainda nao.= No he does not go even though no.

Praque custa todo.= For what does everything costs.

Quando vai baixar o preco?= When will it come down the price?

Por alto eu estremeco!= For high I shake!

Nao tenho moito dinheiro.= I don't have much money.

Pra pagar um caseiro dos jardim.=To pay it handmade of the garden.

Que acho assim nadinha e peor.= I think like this nothing is worse.

Nada mais melhor todo custa.= Nothing more better everything costs.

Em na vida todo acaba resplandezido.=
Everything in life finishes resplended.

Mais nao coibida.=No more cohibited.

08/29/08

Rechazo De Mi Familia =
Rejection Of My Family

Nunca pensé que iba a detestar a mis tios,tias, primos, primas, sobrinos y sobrinas. =I never thought I would hate my uncles, aunts, cousins and nephews and nieces. Que ellos les lambiaban el culo a mi cabron cu~nado.=That they would be kissing ass to my asshole brother-in-law. El rechazo de mi familia del lado materno y paterno es una bofetada para mi me llena de odio. = The rejection of my family on the maternal and paternal side is a blow to my face that fills me with hate. Estoy deprimido, desconsolado. I am depressed, unconsoled. Me siento vulnerable y dolido que me traicionaron.= I feel vulnerable and hurt that they betrayed me . Ellos nunca me quisieron enseñar sus verdaderos colores.= They never wanted to show me their true colors.

Cuando sea alguien en la vida los voy a enterrar vivos en vida.= When I become something big in life, I will bury them alive in life. Voy hacer mi propia familia y mis amistades. = I will make my own family and friends.Cuando llegue al poder voy hacer la vida de mis enemigos en cuadritos.= When I rise to power I will make my enemies lives a living hell. No entiendo lo que me esta pasando estoy enravietado.= I don't understand what is happening I am enraged. Estoy ciego estoy en guerra del pie al ca~non. = I am blind, I am in a state of war with my foot to the canon.

04/19/23

Roca Verde = Green Rock

Umas rocas verdes perto mar.= There are
some green rocks near the ocean.

Sempre andamos pra falar. = We are always ready to talk.

A natureza que beleza.= Nature is a beauty.

A beira mar sinto a pintar o pinto.= Seaside I feel like painting I paint.

Quem me pode dizer que faco pra valer?= Who
can tell me what I can do to value?

Moitas coisas lindas que vejo ainda.= Many
beautiful things that I even see.

Roca verde juntas as rocas da praia e como eu que saia.= Green
rock together as the rocks of the beach and like I that I go out.

Vejo todo bonito que tem a natureza pra mim e uma fortaleza.= I
see everything beautiful that has nature for me and a fortress.

Belos horizontes do verdor uma forca com ardor.=
Beautiful horizons of green a force with ardor.

Temos fervor da vida pela mar e natureza.= We have
fervor of life towards the sea and nature.

Somos gente com amor todos sem dor.= We
are people with love all without hurt.

11/18/09

Rabia=Rage

Que rabia me da estoy fregado hago todo apurado.= What
rage it gives me I am screwed doing everything hurried up.

Nada de descanso soy rebelde no manso.=Nothing
of rest I am a rebel not meek.

La rabia en labia.= The rage in glibness.

No se me quita el coraje tengo mucha tarea sin equipaje.= It doesn't
take away the anger with much homework without baggage.

Me vuelven loco de lo mucho a lo poco.= They
drive me crazy from much to little.

Con la faena sin sabor de hierba buena.=With
the chore without the flavor of mint.

Enojado pero no callado.=Angry but not quiet.

Me viene en mente de repente.=It comes to me in spur of the moment.

disgustes clemente.= dislike gracious.

So Agora = I Am Now

Muncho afito el Dio prosedyo. El me fujo kon su manika a un luguar ke espesifika. Nadika mis alikas bolaron a los luguares de los rikachones ande la djente famosa. So celibater sin esposa sin mente. Afito el milakro sakro ke tuvi i yo anduvi. Mashala ansi es ke la terapia tuvo livyanes. Tengo kompanyeros musafires ala diestra o siniestra al roves. Dimi ken es. Yo so agora sin mi sinyora. = Much happened The lord proceeded. He helped me flee with his little hand to a place that he specified. Nothing my little wings flew to places of rick people where the famous people. I am single without a wife in mind. The sacred miracle I had and wondered. GOD be willing it is therapy had relief. I have companions visitors from right to left and backwards.Tell me who it is. I am without my woman.

02/04/23

Salió El Sol = The Sun Came Out

Salió el sol sobre las montañas de Santa Mónica Parque Nacional.= The sun came out over the mountains of Santa Monica National Park. Veo los árboles y césped donde quiera.= I see trees and grass wherever. El cielo despejado con un arroyuela.= Clear skies with a brook. Un paisaje hermoso con muchos pájaros y ardillas.= A lavish countryside with birds and squirrels. Una barranca con su ca~non andando un gara~non.= A ravine with a canyon riding a stud. La naturaleza es belleza para mi.= Nature is beauty for me. Me cura y perdura así.= It cures me and endures like this. Las plantas dan oxigeno aun no naci primogtenito. = The plants give oxygen even though I was not born the firstborn. Ver las cordilleras de la vista inspira sin ser narcisista. Hay más gente ahora detente.= There is more people now stop.

03/11/23

Saint Patrice = Saint Patrick

Le journe Saint Patrice tous les gens d'Irlande se habillent les robes vertes et parader.=The good day of Saint Patricks all the people of Ireland dress in green clothes and parade. Se manger et boire du boeuf-de Mai et bière. =They eat and drink the corned beef and drink beer. Les gens dansent beaucoup avec l'île emeraude chance de Irlandaise.= The people dance a lot with the emerald isle luck of the Irish.Il ya beaucoup de bandes de cornemuse.= There many bagpipe bands. Mon arriere grand pere etait Irlandaise et Juif Espagnol. = My great great grandfather was an Irish and Spanish Jew. J'écris des liens familiaux en Irlande. =I write of the familial attachments in Ireland. Je suis attaché à la langue et à la culture.=I am attached to the language and culture.

03/17/23

So = I Am

Yo so l'esperanza del djorno ken non tengo sodjorno kez komo soborno.=I have the hope that the day which i don't have sojourn is like a bribe. la bida dyo su naser el plazer. = Life gave its birth to pleasure. Por miyo de mi tiyo es ermano mi on de mi madre.= For mi of my uncle is the brother of my mother. Ansi es mi famiya aspero endjuntar el aunar de relasiones de sangre algo sakro.= Like this my family I await to rejoin the union of relations of blood of something sacred. yo vengo sin fumar el tabako es un tutun sin savor a asukar. = I come without smoking tabacco it is a tobac without flavor to sugar. Munchos kon sus chapeos fumando el tabak Kubano. = There are many with their hats smoking the Cuban Tabacco. A la izla del Karibe aspera la plaj ke veygo munchas aguas mavis. = To the Carribean Isle I wait for the beach that I see much blue waters. Yo no me syento blu de yorar komo L'Amerika dal Norte = I don't feel the blues to cry like North America. So ken so naika manko la djaketa en el mar karibenyo.l= I am someone I am not lacking nothing the jacket in the Carribbean. El diya sta luzyo komo los ojos de mi mujer blanka kabeyo biondo i ojikos blu. =The day is beautiful like the eyes of my white woman blonde hair and blue little eyes. A las kanariyas de Tenerife vo kon mis aguelos avlando i kaminando. = To the Canarys of Tenerife I go with my grandparents talking and walking.

03/31/23

Sinagoga= Synagogue

Yo vo ala sinagoga ke yamo esnoga en chabbat.= I go to the synagogue that I call esnoga in shabbat. Dezde leshos de Rabat.= From afar of Rabat. Vo a San Diego a Ohr Shalom en chabbat.= I go to San Diego to Ohr Shalom in Shabbat. Ma a Tiferet Israel en alhad a San Carlos.= But I go to Tiferet Israel on Sunday to San Carlos.

Para ambezar djudezmo en kal diya de Alhad.= To learn Judaism in schul the day of sunday.

Primo el Kulto a la kehila diya de chabbat.= First worship of the temple of saturday.

Todos d'estos nomvres de sinagoga.= All these names for synagogue.

Yo me vo el fin de la semana a la snoga.= I go to the end of the week to the synagogue.

Agora vo ser kontente stando kon mi djente.= Now I will be happy with being with my people.

Espiritualamente vo al templo ansi yo me asendo la neshama.= Spiritually I go to the temple like this I am lighting my soul.

Komo estar en kaza la kamareta en flama.= It's like being in the bedroom a flames.

11/17/09

Scordato= Forgotten

Perché io scordato quasi tutto mi Italiano.= When
I have forgotten almost all my Italian.

Me manca la pratica.= I lack practice.

Per non avere qualcuna persona per parlare Italiano.=
For there is not a person to speak Italian.

Non ha sempre l'opportunità di parlare.= There
is not always the opportunity to speak.

E difficile per me.= It is difficult for me.

Io amo moltissimo le lingue straniere.= I love
the foreign languages very much.

Io preferisco studiare e imparare una lingua straniera.=
I prefer to study and learn one foreign language.

Io vuoi della vita che non dimenticare di me.=
I want of that life not forget me.

Mai più lasciare i miei lingui.= Never do I want to leave my languages.

Soltanto andiamo a le scuole o computer per imparare
Italiano.=Only we go to the schools or computer to learn Italian.

Per la musica io imparo molto sempre ascolto.=
For the music I learn much always listen.

11/18/09

Sacro Y Profano=Sacred And Profane

Sacro y profano está en el pantano.= Sacred
and profound is in the jungle.

Todo apunta hacia a DIOS.= Everything points toward GOD.

Los ojos ven dos a DIOS.= The eyes are looking at GOD.

Una cosa que no es desastrosa.= One thing is not disasterful.

La vida cotidiana sin lo espiritual no es especial.=Daily
life is not spiritual nor special.

Fe en DIOS seguía el tiempo medieval sin un costal.=Faith
in GOD followed medieval time without a load.

Sagrado es dia honrado de esto no he escapado.=
Sacred is honored day of this I have not escaped.

No es religión si no determinación de ser un feligrés de dos pies.= It
is not religion but determination of being a worshiper with two feet.

Sacro y profano van de mano a mano no en vano.=
Sacred and profane go hand in hand not in vain.

Con libros sagrados mi mente bien a sacado.=With sacred
books in mind well has been taken out.keeps on stoki

Es barrer y limpiar los pecados con la escoba.= To
sweep and mop the sins with the broom.

Ahora miramos diáconos,Rabinos,pastores,Ulemas,sacerdotes
de cada rito con su credo lo sacro y profano.=Now we
see deacons,rabbis,pastors,Ulemas,priests of each
rite with their creed the sacred and profane.

Gracias a DIOS de antemano.= Thanks to GOD beforehand.

Solo la gracia es para un sano.= The grace is for a healed one.

08/12/20

Smoking

I must quit smoking.

Because I'm soaking.

To quit is life to end strife.

I see the mend in quitting smoking end.

It's all in the breath addictive like meth.

I know I must stop I'm human I not a bot.

01/26/21

St Patricks

Top o the morn to you.Where is your color green on Shamrocks
and Leprechauns including Banshees during a Caileadh night.Luck
of the Irish out of sight with a pot of Gold in the light. Corned beef
and cabbage with Irish cream coffee flavored with mint chocolate.
Parades Galore painting the river green,men in kilts,bagpipes a
blaring a whole lot of people staring. IF you are not telling the
truth you are kissing the blarney stone. People all over dancing
the Irish jig, tap dancing with black shoes. March 17th the
National Holiday of in Ireland when it became a Christian nation.
Traditionally a Catholic sensation. Eire guire gwitch/Erin go brach!

03/20/21

Sius Plau=Please

El cel blau.= The blue sky.

Perdoni sius plau.=Sorry please.

Jo vull una noia bell.= I want a beautiful girl.

Molt lluny non puny.= Much far not fist.

Sefarad I la Shoah=Spain And The Holocaust

Sefard i la shoah

Mazal tov a ti mi amado.= Good fortune to you my beloved.

Hitch nada para ti demazalado.=Nothing
nothing for you unfortunate one.

Mozotros semos munchos en el olokausto.=
We are many in the Holocaust.

Ma pokos avagar ke kedimos bivos.= But few
little by little that were left alive.

Ande esta Selanik,Monastir,Rodes.= Where is
Thesaloniki, Monastir and Rhodes.

Ya no biven ayi los muestros debaldes.= Now
they don't live there our own for free.

Agora en la diaspora.= Now in the diaspora.

Aresentados ma no fruchiguados.= Arranged but not fruitful.

Ma amenguados.= But diminished.

Tia Panchita = Aunt Francis

Querido Tia Panchita = Dear Aunt Francis.

Yo te extraño mucho , tanto cari~no te tengo. = I miss you much,with great tenderness I have for you. Recuerdo los consejos que me dabas ahora ya no estás conmigo = I remember your advice that you gave me now you are not with me.

Tuviste alzheimer y te olvidaste de mí. = You had Alzheimers and forgot about me. Te violentadas porque sufrías mucho.= You got violent because you suffered a lot. Así es que te escucho. = That is how I hear you. Algun dia cuando muera te volveré a ver. = Someday when I die I will see you again. Estoy pensando en ti. = I am thinking of you. Yo tuve ese lazo contigo desde pequeño como un sueño . = I had a tie with you since I was a little one like a dream. A las cinco me engríe contigo.= At five I bonded with you. Eras muy religiosa y hablabas de DIOS . = You were religious and talked of GOD. No hay momento en que yo no te recuerde. = There is not a moment that I don't remember. Fuiste como mi tercera abuela y al mismo tiempo mi tía abuela. = You were my third grandma at the same time you were my grand aunt. Los consejos me los dabas cada día. = The advice you gave me each day. Yo se reconocerte aunque no puedo verte.= I recognize you even though I can't see you. Descansa en paz si tienes el cielo ya ganada. = Rest in peace you have won heaven now. Te quiero y te espero. = I love you and wait for you.

02/10/23

The Rose Painting

The blossoms represent my sweetness or success. The spines symbolize my suffering for years. The blue sky is hope. The brown earth to be grounded. The leaves are the growth of old to new life without strife. It gives me perspective to distribute the cards on the table of that which I'm able. From chaos to stability. Nothing is black and white. There are different shades of gray in delight. From which I gain insight. To turn at night to the moon. I will croon. I was not born with a silver spoon.Always looking at my rose which strikes a pose.

02/16/23

Traumatized

I slammed doors,got angry and broke things on the floor traumatizing my nephews and my niece. I drove violently while my mother was inside. I verbally attacked my second generation nieces.I threatened my cousin with death threats. That is how I taumed my family member's that they are traumatized. It is not easy for me to take responsibility for my actions. My family has turned against me. Now they don't want to forgive me. I am angry too because they did things to me that I have not forgotten. I have a lot of inner pain as a result.

04/19/23

The Way

Lord show me the way to grow in the faith.

I know you are my say to the wreath. GOD tell me how to better myself.

I don't want to give up lord Jesus. I trust in the holy spirit to inspire. The hour is dire at night I sleep to retire. Only with your love from above. I survive for a holy way to strive. If we sin hell is the dive. But to repent is money well spent. To God our prayers without lament. Lord you bless me do not stress me. I sing to my joy better than a toy.

The Seasons

The seasons come and go.

In three month's increments they show

Fall, Winter, Summer and Spring.

It makes me want to sing.

In the fall we bundle up.

Keep close to the fire.

Drinking hot tea on the tea cup.

A chimney sweep we hire.

In winter I chop wood to a splinter.

We gather near the chimney for warmth for a sprinter.

In summer I drive a hummer to keep cool
like the drummer it is no ummer.

Spring I can ring a bell.

While I walk in the park not after dark without a spark.

By and by they come in threes just like counting trees.

Seasons greetings.

Tis the season not to be fleeting.

The seasons with reasons.

11/24/09

The Days

The days when we have no one to talk to.

We are cooped up, busy and there is no one to talk to
because they are working or going to school.

I can't complain like a fool.We are so needy sometimes it seems
greedy. I have to find things to do. Sometimes I don't have a clue.

The monotony of life with strife. It's so very unpredictable.
Sometimes I get inexcusable. The moments of life are immutable.

I must keep up with plenty to do. I have moments of great silence. I
die in ambivalence. I scratch my head which seems filled with lead.

Life's cruciality without someone to talk to disparity. I am slumped.

12/24/19

Transisyon = Transition

Agora yo vo di transisyon. = Now I go by transition.

Diya en diya al korason por menester de salu.= Day
in day to the heart for the need of health.

El DIO ke me abedigua ankora mijior. = May G-D help me still better.

Ke me kita el dolor.= That takes away my pain.

Non ay komo muestro DIO!. = There is no one like our G-D!

Ke ayuda kadal diya: komo los zinganos kantar siguirya.=
To help each day : like the gypsies sing siguirilla.

Di un lugar a otro para ver el enkontro.= From one
place to the other to see the encounter.

Adelantre vamos a topar el muestro ogar. =
Forward we go to find our abode.

Solo esta vida save el porke munchas kosikas yo no se. = Only
this life knows the why of many little things I don't know.

Trokamos el mazal kon el djugar. = We change luck with the play.

Los rekodros vyenen presto la memorya menesto.=
The memories come quick the memory I need.

Si diya es maraviya andamos kon ti. = Yes
day is a marvel we go with you.

Todo savi non es komo kumer el agave.= All is
known it is not like eating the aloe.

Si la vida troka i va di transisyon en transisyon. = If life
changes and goes from transition in transition.

Me vyeni fuerte la emosyon. = It brings a strong emotion to me.

01/09/20

Temecula

I never thought I would live in your midst. I passed you by oh my. Now after back and forth I am entrenched. How ironic the twin cities like National City and Chula Vista its Temecula and Murrieta.

No, I don't have Elisabetta. Never imagined in a million years I would be here today. Temecula is its way. So many options in San Diego.

01/21/20

The Vale Of Myst

I see the myst in the vale above Temecula. What lands or seas does it lead to. Shrouded in mystery this may seem but always wondering what lies ahead it goes to the west coast to beautiful beaches.I can't imagine the routes that these mountains cover. It is laced with green velvet so it seems natural.

03/12/20

The New Normal

The new normal what is it?Gone are the days of dining in now its takeout,drive thru or delivery. Today you have to wear a mask in public or you can't go inside establishments. So many laments. As you go it's an injury to personal freedom.Now you can't go into the store freely but have to wait in line at the drop of a dime taking time. I feel the changing rhymes of the times. It's surrealistic yet not mystic.The pandemic has changed the epic of the cycle. Churches are closed as n opposed. Only bars, restaurants and stores galore. Not even schools or libraries open, it's like I have lost a token. Coronavirus covid19 is our new reality of fear, not so dear sweat a tear. Now you know it's everything behind closed doors at home shocking. There are not many places for your faces.

08/12/20

Thanksgiving

I spent it with mom and Uncle Joe. I was not a pro. We had turkey,macaroni , sald, eggnog , coffee, juice and water. I gave thanks. Why bother? I didn't eat baked potatoes and there were no tomatoes. I ate cranberry sauce which was bitterly glad. I'm not a switch hitter. I had a place to go for Thanksgiving. I keep on receiving and I don't go on grieving. I say I thank G-d not my bod. I am forever grateful, not spiteful. I have so many blessings. I have a mom, family, pension, roof over my head. This is how I know I am not made of lead. I take nothing for granted.

11/27/20

Time

Time is what we have in short supply without getting high.

We can't do everything in 24 hours.

We have to space out what we do.

Time is of essence, especially a heavenly presence.

Time is a commodity in short spurts that we can't take back.

It takes time to get right on track.

We even look for ways to prolong a task or lesson through time.

So we take it easy, long and slow dance till we get tired then its time.

How do we measure it?

It stretches from seconds to minutes to hours to
days to nights to weeks to months to years.

I have been wondering about things over time. Even
food is slow cooked for several minutes to hours like
roasting a pig in a sand oven it takes time.

Time is infinite yet finite for it ends and does not come back.

Once time finishes that is all they can do.
Therefore,Time stretches but it ends.

01/22/21

Tet Chino = Chinese Tet

Dragones, linternas, rojo y oro las se~nales del A~no Nuevo Chino.=
Dragons,lamps,red and gold the signs of the Chinese New Year.

Hasta bebidas de ciruela hecho en vino.= Upto
beverages of plum made into wine.

Pasteles dulces de arroz son hechos para
comer.= Moon cakes made to eat.

Todos los Orientales lo celebran no solo
China,Vietnam,Cambodia,Filipinas,Guam,Japon,Laos
etc.= All the Orientals celebrate it not only
China,Vietnam,Cambodia,Philipines,Guam,Japan,Laos etc.

Se come mucha fruta.= A lot of fruit is eaten.

Se prenden el incienso en altares. = Incense is lit up in the altars.

Se hace el lechon Oriental,pollo rostisado y arroz con brocoli e res.=
Oriental pig roast, rotisserie chicken and rice with brocoli and beef.

Se toma mucho te.= Much tea is drunken.

Adoran en los altares venerando a los antepasados.=
They worship in the altars venerating the ancestors.

Hacen adivinaciones para un buen presagio.= They
make adivination for a good auspice.

Todo esto me imagino para el a~no Nuevo Chino.=
I imagine for the Chinese New Year.

02/12/21

Thanksgiving

What do we give thanks for?

The Indians taught the settlers how to survive in the winter.

Without chopping a wood splinter/

Pilgrims rock is considered the beginning of the end.

Who will they for Native America tend.

Its mixed feelings all wrapped up on one.

Saying come on hun.

We remember turkeys,pumpkins,corn,fish,deer,game,cranberries
and clam chowder.

In Canada it is celebrated on a different day.

The 22nd on the fourth Thursday of November
is Thanksgiving in the U.S.A.

In Canada its Thanksgiving Day on the second Monday of October 8th.

So many good and bad things happened after Thanksgiving.

Yet at meal time we say what we are grateful
for with family and friends.

We gather around the dinning room.

Like were flying on a broom.

Terra = Earth

Nesta terra foi movida.= This earth was moved.

Um dia.= One day.

Um temblor.= Like a earthquake.

Que nos fai teror.=That makes us feel terror.

Todo isto pra mim.= All this for me.

Como uma revolucao um movimento.= It is
like a revolution, a movement.

Este nao foi meu pensamento dentro o corpo.=
This was not my thinking inside the body.

Sentia na movida olhava minha agua.= I felt the move see my water.

Esto uma maravilha de Castilha.= This was a marvel of Castile.

Tiempo= Time

Hay una eternidad cuando no se hace nada.=
There is an eternity when nothing is done.

Pero si nos ocupamos no hay para que queda.= If we
keep busy there is nothing for that to be left.

Como bailar el Chachacha.= Like dancing the Chachacha.

Una rutina sin espina cada dia es maravilla.= A
routine without a spine each day is a marvel.

Como la noche su esplendor es decir en Hebreo dorldor.= It
is like the night its splendor is to say in Hebrew dorldor.

De generacion en generacion.= From generation to generation.

Pero si el tiempo se nos acaba.= But the time it finishes.

ahava olam amor al mundo.= Love of the world.

The Bird

The bird in its cage.

The bird passes each day.

Awaiting the return of its master.

When the master sees it it greets it with caring.

The bird coos as it gives a kiss.

Letting him pet it as usual up and down.

In and out the bird climbs out of its cage.

It receives its treat of peanuts.

Alas the bird is content.

No more gloom.

No more sadness.

The bird relishes its attention.

Content and happy.

Una Rosa= A Rose

Una rosa le quiero dar a Yizel.= A rose I want to give to Giselle.

Pero lejos está de mi en Altar,Sonora,Méjico de donde vino
mi nana.= But far away she is from me in Altar,Sonora,Mexico
from which came forth my grandmother.

Aunque lejos está cuando estemos juntos le daré una rosa.=Even
from afar she is when we are together I will give her a rose.

Un amor comprendido sin decir un despido.= A
love understood without saying goodbye.

El Flechazo tardó en llegar por cupido pero a Dios le pido.=
The love flame was late in arriving for cupid but G-d I ask.

No importa el tiempo o lejanía estar con ella es mi maravilla.=Time
does not matter nor distance to be with her is my marvel.

Todo o nada en un dia.= All or nothing in one day.

Sayana porque vives día a día es que yo no te despida.= Sayane
why won't you live day to day is it that I bid you farewell.

Un hola te espero es a ti que yo quiero.= A
hello I await you, that is who I love.

Una rosa de durazno te quiero dar eres tu mi paladar.= A
peach rose I want to give you that you are my palate.

Un azar y azucena no hay nada que me condena.= A chance
and madonna lily for me there is no prison sentence.

Por una frontera es lo que yo quiera.= For a frontier is what I want.

Los lazos de arraigamiento nos unen mi nana vino de Altar
ahora tu vienes a mi vida.=The ties of rooting that unites us
my grandma came from Altar now you come into my life.

Soltero ya no quise a ti te tengo desde ahora que vengas
en buena hora.= Single I did not want now its you
that I have now may you come in a good hour.

02/16/20

Up In Smoke

Next day so I made a way to smoke.. Its not an
embra smoking in a trace.ce to stop

Up in smoke, quit smoking or you choke. It's not easy to give up
smoking for you to grow choking if it keeps on stoking. I gave up
exercising and couldn't breathe, quit smoking cold turkey without
eating beef jerky. I know what made me quit without having a fit.
Smoking is so addictive you have to use mind over matter in order to
stop. Smoking is a chemical dependency. It's not not nice breathing
and not even teething. I was exercising and couldn't breathe the
next day so I made a way to stop smoking.I see it causes disease
which is not a tease. COPD is not seeing #D.Give up the smoking
craze to give it up in a heart attack daze . It's not an embrace to
stop in a trace. Next day I made a way smoke.Fiinally I gave up
cigarettes without getting turrets. It's a wise move to stop smoking.

08/13/20

Vacio=Empty

No se que hacer en el vacío solo hacer mi cama, estudiar, escribir, cambiarme, ba~narme y limpiarme.= I don't know what to do in the emptiness only make my bed, study, write, change, bathe and clean myself up.

Ya que la gente y yo no podemos tener contacto por lo del corona virus.= Now that people and I cannot have contacto because of the corona virus.

Espero que se acabe esta peste tarde o temprano.= I wait for this pandemic to be over sooner or later.

Por mientras estamos en cuarentena aislados en nuestros casas.= For now we are in quarentine isolated in our homes.

Solo Dios sabe cuando las cosas vendran a la normalidad.= Only G-D knows when the things will come back to normal.

Por lo tanto estamos en las manos de Dios.= For now we are in G-Ds hands.

No puedo entender la crisis tal como es ahora.= I can't understand the crisis how it is now.

Espero que descubran una cura para la epidemia mundial los scientificos y doctores de los gobiernos de las naciones.=I hope they discover a cure for the world epidemic the scientists and doctors of the different national goverments.

Solo Dios sabe lo que acontecera y que sera de la humanidad.= Only G-d knows what will occur and what will be of humanity.

Todo esta en peligro hasta que haiga una cura y se ponga fin al vacio.= Everthing is in danger until there is a cure and there is an end to the vacuum.

03/17/20

Veterans Day

It's not bad because I brought flowers for my dad. Thank GOD he's
not Brad nor am I crying I'm not sad carnations I put be his headstone
no lamentations to this somber tones. It's as if there are no more
drones, only graves in Miramar National Cemetery all white .My
dads letter is engraved. There are so many people, crowded cars
there except you can't see the stars only at night. closed it is the
site I will not hang around for fright. I come there in the daylight.
I remember Dad fought in Vietnam. My father was at E3 like me
but he was higher than a noncom. I often go to his grave when I
behave. Me and mom bring him flowers lower than the towers.

12/03/20

Vacio = Void

Mi mente se siente como un basurero vacio.=
My mind feels like an empty trashcan.

Esta agotada mi mente porque la inspiracion se me ha ido.=
It is tired my mind because the inspiration has left me.

Todo o nada a quien se dispara.= All or nothing to whom I shoot.

Hay muchos lazos en mis poemas con muchos esquemas.= There
are many attachements in my poems with many schemes.

Yo aprendo de mis inspiraciones que me laten de mil razones.=
I learn of my inspirations which beat a thousand reasons.

Es un enigma faltar el escribir para mi un decir.= It
is an enigma to lack the writing for a saying.

Tantos momentos de vida el recorrido saludar el dia a
Dios despido.= So many moments of life the memory
lane to greet the day to God I say goodbye.

Mi Corazón tiene uso de razon. = My heart has use of reason.

Necesito una vacacion para llenarme de ilusiones con
revelaciones es todo o nada. = I need a vacation for me to
fill up with ilusions with revalations it is all or nothing.

Las dos partes de mi cara el lado feliz como una lumbriz y la otra de
tristeza con su baja raiz.= The two sides of my face the happy side
like a glowworm and the other side of sadnss with it's lower root.

Un enigma contundente que viene paso a paso de repente.=
An enigma blunt that comes step by step all of a sudden.

A veces no se lo que tengo en mi mente pero noe es una serpiente.=
At times I don't know what I have in mind but it is not a serpent.

Garrotin engarrotado este cuento se ha acabado.=
Cudgel clubbed this story has finished.

01/19/21

Vento=Wind

O vento gris que tem o dia sombrio porque o sol não está lá fora.=The gray wind which the day has is somber because the sun is not outside.

Vate embora a tristeza da natureza.=Go although the sadness of nature.

Muitos sozinhos estamos todos no mundo.=Many alone we are in the world.

Covid-19 e que escureceu o dia com a gente distanciada
6 pés com as cubrebocas.=Covid-19 is that darkened
day with people distanced 6 feet with face masks.

Se os juntarmos é por Zoom para não ter máscaras e
distância entre a gente.= We got together and by Zoom
for not to have masks and distance between people.

Tudo isso e a leccao,igreja,escola,juntas sociais ainda tudo
que fazemos juntos.= All that is a lesson, church, school,
social gatherings even though everything we do together.

Sinto que isto em uma pisadela mau.= I feel this is a bad dream.

Não temos concertos em vivo mais por Zoom no mais.
= We don't have concerts live but by Zoom.

Não jantamos dentro dos restaurantes e por comer fora
o pedido pra levar a casa. = We don't dine inside the
restaurants and eat outside or ask for take out.

Sempre a aceitar nossa realidade que e outra demais. =
Always we accept our reality that it is another thing.

Acho que vai definir isso de covid-19.=I wonder
when this of covid-19 will finish.

Esperamos voltar a normalidade.=We wait for normality to return.

A vacina vai trocar tudo pra nós que voltamos sair agora.= The
vaccine will change everything for us to return to go outside now.

O vento gris se vai voltar em dia de sol com alegria.=The
gray wind will return to a day of sun with happiness.

01/19/21

Vida=Life

Que es mi vida para estar so~nando o el lema de estar cantando? =
What is my life that is dreaming or the watchword of to be singing.
Vida que es lo que decides para mi me das vueltas que no quiero.=
Life what is it you decide for me you give me turns I do not want. Ni
cumples con lo que deseo. = You don't fulfill with what I want. No
me dejas por la paz siempre mudandome al compas.= You don't
leave me in peace always moving me to the compass. Interfieres
en mi conversion Judia y ahora con mi manejo.= You interfere in my
Jewish conversion and now with my driving. Ya basta con el despecho
dejame vivir tranquilo por la paz.= Thats enough with the spite let
me live tranquil in peace. Dejame ser yo mismo sin un abismo.=Let
me be me myself without an abyss. Borron y cuenta nueva para
principiar.= Clean slate and new beginning to start. Vida dejame vivir
en paz.= LIfe let me live in peace. Mi corazon esta harto de Temecula.=
My heart is sick of Temecula. Quiero volver a San Diego al final de
todo.= I want to return to San Diego at the end of everything.

What Shall I do

What shall I do today or tomorrow. Sad, not happy but sorrow.
In case of a rainy day don't borrow. I will try nor be shy I will be
good not sly. Somehow, I feel the thrill with no shrill. How many
is there any? I know but who do I stow. Chill out bro. I don't
smoke malborough. I feel like the twilightzone without saying
pogue mahone. My name is not Jerome I have a home.

02/27/23

When I Greet The Sun

When I greet the sun; I see cloulds of days gone past. It's a blast from
the past. I see the birds, insects and squirrels. I see the flowers and
the trees in the backyard. I enjoy the fresh air. To me it's fair. I Look
forward to skies then I see the clouds. The rains come and go but
the land remains. A huge backyard to a composing bard. I am Sam.
The small palms I enjoy but are no toy. I see green, brown and black,
green environment stack. There is no firmament or lament. My time
here is spent. To G-D I turn to repent. As is all of nature to nurture. I
greet the sun to have fun. I wish for a forest g en waiting to mend. I
am happy as can be without the sea. I greet the sun waiting a ton.

04/07/20

Washington's Birthday

You are the father of our country.Honest about chopping
down your neighbors cherry tree You said "

I cannot tell a lie I chopped down the cherry tree." You fought for
our freedom against tyranny. No taxation without representation.

You started the continental army and declared the
Confederation of the thirteen colonies.

You helped in making our constitution. Fourth of July 1776 is when we
declared independence. So much has changed in several generations.

You were jack of all trades and master of some. You fought well for
the British and America. You adopted a child or were you wild. You
amaze me with your life. Your place Mount Vernon became famous.

You were self educated unlike your brothers and father. Your wife
was Martha, you had no children of your own. What an irony.

02/15/21

Words

An illusion.

A good idea.

Seismic pitch punches.

Secrets to captivate.

Slowed and levelled.

To lug around.

When

When I return to my cocoon it will feel like I'm on the moon. Back to teach my Ladino Class just like I did in the past. To return to Visions is to live again. When I go back to school it will be cool.

To take the bus and the trolley has been in my mind. San Diego is where I unwind. My soul is at peace here more than anywhere in the world. I'm not a squirrel.When I left Temecula I started to breathe. I smile with my teeth.

Xirei A Este, Oeste, Norte, Sur= I Turned To The East, West, North, South

Eu xirei as catro direccions este, oeste,norte, e sur de
Temecula e Murrieta.= I turned to the four directions east,
west, north, and south of Temecula and Murrieta.

Sentindo as emocions que ven do meu corazon.=
Feeling the emotions that come from my heart.

As leccions que percebi e comendo unha hamburguesa,
refresco e batatas fritas.= The lessons that I perceived
and eating a hamburger, soda and french fries.

Xirei por una hora caxi de trinta a corenta cinco minutos
voltei a casa.= I turned for almost an hour of thirty
to forty five minutes before I returned home.

Foi as monta~nas e vale depois a cidade en diferente dirección.= I went
to the mountains and valley after the city in a different direction.

Xirando polo automoveis e a xente cami~nando e andando a bicicleta.=
Turning through the autos and the people walking and riding a bicycle.

Un cami~no ande por meu andar a coche dependendo meus
sentimentos da ceibe polo ar con as ventanas abertas do meu
coche.= A road to go for my driving the car depending on my
sentiments of freedom through the open windows of my car.

Non estacionei por ali beixando o ver de dous campos e vale en
direccions a os Anxeles mais non terminando de conduzir meu coche.=
I did not park down there seeing the look at the camps and the valley
in directions to Los Angeles but not finishing the driving of my car.

Gostei moi meu andar vou lembrar mi~na andanza.=
I liked my going to remember my wandering.

Ver a natureza foi un prazer pra min hoxe.= To
see nature was a pleasure for me today.

04/27/20

Yo Me Enfade = I Got Angry

Me enfade de vivir la vida de joda.= I got angry of life the life of fuck it.

Encima esta mi familia.= On top is my family.

Yo ya no puedo mas con la carga.= I can't take the load.

Quiero mi libertad a toda cuesta.= I want my liberty at all cost.

Me despierto de la siesta.=I wake up from my nap.

Abrumado estoy porque no descanso.=Overwhelmed
I am because I have no rest.

No quiero ni voy para el dia de hoy.= I don't
want nor do I go for the day of today.

Vivo desapercibido como yo me retiro= I live unnoticed like I retire.

Quisiera una solucion que es la evolucion.=I
want a solution what is the evolution.

De mi vida cotidiana ya no es mi manzana.=Of
my everyday life it is not my apple.

No tengo espacio ni privacia como si perdi la mercancia.= I don't
have space nor privacy it's like I have lost the merchandise.

Hasta cuando vendra el fin a mi problema.= Till
when will the end come to my problem.

Ni acuarela ni esquema.=Nor watercolor or scheme.

Estoy enfadado como DIOS a dado.=I am angry like GOD has given.

Quiero respirar y no puedo por mucho e poco me quedo.=
I want to breathe and I cant much or little I stay.

2/3/93

Corazo~ng Esperanzao.= My Hopefull Heart

Me~ngdaz corazo~ng eta lle~no e Ezpera~ngza.=
My heart is full of hope.

De~nde er ora la xe~ngte te~nra xambruzia po la paz.=
Why it was time the people had hunger for peace.

Poquei po o~ng mome~ngto ay paz.= Because
for one moment there is peace.

Cua~ndo Dibe xizo er mu~ngdo.= When GOD made the world.

Er puzo a Xezu.= He put Jesus.

Quei lo quei se se~ngtia~ng zoloz etaba~ng acompa~naoz.=For
those who felt alone would be accompanied.

2/3/93

Ir pa? Ir pa? Ir pa?= Go Where? go where go where

O quei zera e mem ir pa?= What will be of me and where can I go?

Me~ngdaz africzio~ng e ma puro chungo.=
Mi aflicción es más mal puro.

Me~ngdaz e ze~ngtio xi~ndama.=I feel terror.

Dibe camela me~ndaz alibio.= God desires my relief.

2/4/93

Xaumar Ta Xaular

Xaumar Ta Xaular.= To Drink And Take

Pa~ni pa xumar.= Water to Drink.

Me~ndi acoradao e mangdi exatico.=I remember my penthouse.

Comia pa xaular cuangdo zeom llac oxusito xaular.=
I ate because I was a baby pig out.

O~nde eta me~ngdaz bibi.= Where s my aunt.

Era mem preparaola oztaro.= She prepared the pot.

Zolo eca mi~nuto.= Only a minute.

Quei ora fuerong cuaber dibuz.= What time was in those days.

Too tei~neng zu angta.= Everything has its end.

2/4/93

Cazao=Married

Me~ngda me e cazao tube do groengroz.=
I am married I had two horses.

~Na e ixo zeom ung perioizta.= Nothing and
children I became a journa ist.

Er xuego e mangdiz via ~Naire e lo gorxio cha~nela.= I
play and my life nobody and the nongypsy knows.

Queca er fezting .= No feast.

2/5/93

Ma Mere = My Mother

Maman ale pour visitemoi.= My mother goes to visit me.

Al L'hôpital que je sante un peu.=To the hospital that I be a little healed.

Quelque chose que je veux un peu.=That thing that I want a little.

Quand je sante mon salut.=When I am healed with health.

Pour un peu aujourd'hui maman comprend.=For
a little today my mother understand.

Partout je fais recouverte mon sanite=Overall
I made a recovery of my health.

2/5/93

Ma Che Tu Vuole?= What Do You Want?

Il giorno ha sole.= The day will be sun.

Sole caldo ma che tu vuole?=The hot sun but what do you want?

Il sole sto cercando.= The sun is near.

Parlame per ancora lo caldo.=Speak to me still I am hot.

Oggi so l'ora e consuelo ma che tu vuole?=Today is the
only hour and consoling but what do you want?

Andiamo a casa sulla mia famiglia!= Let's go home to my family.

In carrozza andiamo.= In a carriage.

2/6/93

Malditos Doctores Traicioneros= Cursed Doctors Betrayers.

Malditos Doctores Traicioneros Sos Naficy,Roundy,Ryan
Jones.=Cursed Doctors are you Naficy,Roundy,Ryan Jones.

Malditos Doctores Traicioneros

Maldigo el día que nacieron.= I curse the day of their birth.

Maldito Doctores Traicioneros

Maldigo su familia y el hospital donde trabajan.= I curse
their family and the hospital where they work.

Malditos Doctores Traicioneros

Me hablaban de curarme pa despues chingarme.= They
spoke to me about curing me to later fuck over me.

Malditos Doctores Traicioneros.

Yo maldigo sus moradas y sus obras.= I curse
your homes and your works.

Malditos Doctores Traicioneros

Son ustedes gente de doble cara.= You are two faced people.

Malditos Doctores Traicioneros

Solo si alguien se les parara harían de su problema en nada.= If only
they would stand in front they would make their problem in nothing.

Malditos Doctores Traicioneros

Encubridores de los crimenes hechos a inocentes.= Cover
ups of the crimes committed against the innocent.

Malditos Doctores Traicioneros

2/26/93

Seguridad=Security

Es mi fe en DIOS.= It is my faith in GOD.

seguridad

Amor de los dos.= Love of the two.

seguridad

Tiempo sana las llagas después de las plagas.= Time
of the healing wounds later of the plagues.

seguridad

Tengo que seguir viviendo.= I must keep living.

seguridad

Y tener razón para estar existiendo.= And to have reason to be existing.

seguridad

Cada etapa de mi vida.= Each phase of my life.

seguridad

Va con la era corrida.= It goes with the ongoing era.

seguridad

Es mi fe en DIOS.=It is my faith in GOD.

seguridad.

2/26/93

Aveugle De La Vie.= Blind of Life

Je me sens une veugle.= I feel like a blind man.

La nuit que Je Me Sentir comme une veugle.=
The night that I will feel like a blind man.

Je me sens une veugle.

J'oublierai la raison de mon existence.=I have
forgotten the reason for my existence.

Je me sens une veugle.

Je ne savais pas pourquoi je réfléchissais'.= I don't know why I reflect.

Je me sens une veugle.

Mon père et ma mère me diront 'faites tout pour votre
santé'.=My father and mother tell me to do for our health.

Je me sens une veugle.

Quel dommage est la solution pour moi.=What
a pity where is the solution for me.

Je me sens un veugle.

Toute la nuit je réfléchi pour mon future.=All
the night I reflect for my future.

Je me sens un veugle

2/7/93

Po Er Prao.= For The Meadow.

Me~ngda e a~ndao.= I have not been.

o~ng er cangria.= In the church.

cong er razhai.= With the priest.

A reza me~ngda birxe~ngzita macarena macarena.=
I pray to the virgen of Macarena, Macarena.

Xi~ndu Xita~no = Hindu Gypsy

Mayor Raxaz Raxput.= Big kings

Maxara~niz= Big Queens

Po er prao= By the meadow.

Me~ngda e a~ngdao.= I have been

O~ng er ca~ngria.= In a church.

Co~ng er Razhai.=With the priest.

Me~ngda a reza ara.= I pray to her.

Birxe~ngzita Macarena.= Virgen Macarena.

Tut ca~ngta com chir chir.= You sing like a bird.

Po Dibe le agradao er rezo.= Because God pleases the prayer.

Queca ay quei zer feli zing o~ng lezti.= There
is no being happy without a tribe.

Xita~no tientez o~n lezti.= Gypsy you have your tribe.

196

2/7/93

Upari baru~na er mimo dibe dica po lo i^noze~nte.= Up in the sky the same GOD watches for the innocents.

Pallo ergraziao tut xaze ca~nud mizericordia.= NonGypsy ungracious you do withcut mercy.

Tutiz boquiar co~ng chungo.= You work with evil.

Pa co~ng lo i~noze~ngte.= With the innocents.

2/8/93

Todos juntos à noite.= Everyone together for the night.

Pra que eu me sinta como um dez.= Why do I feel like a ten.

Todos juntos a noite.

Isto porque eu estou um pouco cheio da esperança.=
It is because I am a little filled with hope.

Todos juntos a noite.

Onde eu posso sentir mais bem agora.=Where I can feel better now.

Todos juntos a noite.

2/8/93

Gooden Habens Uberfrau Deutsche.=Good
afternoon German head woman.

Was ist das?=What is this?

Mein fraulein gooder nacht.= My dear miss good evening.

Was ist das?= What is this?

Mein frau.= My wife

Zu sprechen und fistein.=You speak and understand.

Ich fistein und spreche klein.= I understand and speak a little bit.

2/8/93

Dobriy Dyen= Good Morning

Pazhaloosta.=Please and Your Welcome.

Balshoye Spasiba.=Thank You Very Much.

Da Da.=Yes,Yes.

Nyet.=No.

Da Da.= Yes,Yes.

Dobriy vechor=Good Night.

Pazhaloosta.= Please and Your Welcome.

Dasvidanya=Goodbye.

Da,Da, nyet=Yes,Yes,No

Da,Da,Nyet.=Yes,Yes,No

2/9/93

Amore Di Lontano.= Love Of Far.

Domani Io non ho un amore.= Tomorrow I don't have a love.

Amore Di Lontano

Dietro il cuore.= Inside the heart.

Amore Di Lontano

Domani è il giorno di San Valentino.=Tomorrow
is the day of St. Valentine.

Amore Di Lontano

Amore di lungo miei amori che non stai sulla me.=
Love of long my loves are not here with me.

Amore Di Lontano

Di me cinque amori che non stai sulla me.= Of
me five loves that are not with me.

Amore Di lontano

Gli ragazzas si chiamano Marta & Lucia,Laura & Elizabeta e Maria.=
The girls are called Martha & Lucie,Laura & Elizabeth and Mary.

Amore di lontano

Ma ancora Io canto per la Donna qui si chiama Rozio.=
But still I sing for the lady that is called Rocio.

Amore di lontano

200

2/12/93

Lejos= Far

Lejos esta mi solucion.= Far is my solution.

Lejos

Que me llena de emoción.= That fills me with emotion.

lejos

Estas mi amor mi abuela mi libertad.= You are there
my love, my grandmother, my iberty.

Lejos

Está la flor mi canela mi voluntad.= This is
the flow of my cinnamon,my will.

lejos

Larga es mi situacion.= Long is my situation.

lejos

Es como globo su revolución.= It is like a globe.

lejos.

2/12/93

Sobrinos= Nephews

Tanto espere poder tener mis propios jijos.= I
waited to be able to have my own children.

Sobrinos

Pero el criado decide primero tendré sobrinos.= But
first I create and decide first I will have nephews.

sobrinos

Yo les ense~nare hablar sus idiomas.= I will
teach them to speak languages.

sobrinos

Espa~nol y Alemán serán multilingüe en su iman.= Spanish
and German they will be multilingual in thier faith.

sobrinos

Ojalá que estén allí cuando nazcan.= I hope
that they are there when their born.

sobrinos

Que Yo esté donde estan.= That I be where they are.

2/13/93

Jo Plant Jorn Y Nit.=I Cry day and night.

Jo vull fer llibre com lo ar.=I want to become free like the air.

Mes que mai.=Mor than May.

Jo sentiu encadenat.= I felt enchained.

Jo plant Jorn y nit.

Ara despue molt temp que jo no esto amb meva
família.=Now after much time, I am not with my family.

Jo plant jorn y nit .

Jo vist a me trist.=I seen to me sad.

Jo plant jorn y nit

Cathascu teniu sua llibertat.=Each one has their liberty.

Quan ser jo llibre com un om.=When I am free like the man.

Jo plant jorn y nit.

2/14/93

Recuerdo Mi Juventud.= I Remember My Youth.

Se me vienen las fiestas,reuniones familiares y mis aventuras
en mi memoria.= It comes back to me the parties, family
get togethers and my adventures in my memory.

Recuerdo Mi Juventud

Todos los sue~nos de actor, bailarin,cantautor e
musico salen por alli.= All my dreams of actor, dancer,
singer author and musician come from there.

Recuerdo Mi Juventud

También vienen en mente mis idiomas extranjeros.=
Also come to my mind my foreign languages.

Recuerdo Mi Juventud

Muchas cosas tomé por balde incluyendo el alcalde.=
Many things I took for granted including the mayor.

Recuerdo Mi Juventud

2/14/93

Laura Amor Ilusivo= Laura Elusive Love

Laura tu lejos de mi.=Laura you far from me.

Siempre estaras dentro mi corazón= You will always be in my heart.

Laura Amor Ilusivo

Yo nunca te olvidare siempre te recordaré.= I will
never forget you, I will always remember you.

Laura Amor Ilusivo

Yo me hice civil tu una militar.= I became a civilian you a military.

Laura Amor Ilusivo

Te quiero pero no te puedo soltar aunque eres una militar.=I want
you but I don't want to let you go even though you are a military.

Laura Amor Ilusivo

Me quebraste en dos por esto canta mi voz.= You
broke me in two that's why my voice sings.

Laura Amor Ilusivo

Solo Dios Sabra el me dira.= Only GOD will know what he shall say.

Laura Amor Ilusivo

2/15/93

Ou Est Ma Femme.= Where Is My Woman.

Je ne suis pas une semblance de ma vie.=I
am not a semblance of my life.

Ou est ma femme.

Je crie pour moi.= I believe in myself.

Ou est ma femme.

Je n'ai pas le savoir de mon futur.=I don't know of my future.

Ou est ma femme.

Mon passe' il temps passe'.=My past the time past.

Ou est ma femme.

Ou maintenant ou est la promesse de ma
vie?=Where now is the promise of my life?

Ou est ma femme.

Les années passent.=The years pass.

Ou est ma femme.

Quel dommage que j'ai perdu mon amour!.=What
a pity I have lost my love!

2/16/93

He Perdido Mi Paz= I Have Lost My Peace

Alejado estuve de mi gente entre extra~nos more' = Away
I was from my people between strangers I lived.

He Perdido Mi Paz

Esté foso que han escarbado es mi morada.= These
grave they have dug up is my home.

He Perdido Mi Paz

Es que como yo sufrí la canallada.=It is
because I have suffered to vileness.

He Perdido Mi Paz

Quien mas sera un maldito capataz?= Who else
more will be a cursed head overseer.

He Perdido Mi Paz

Indignado a tal grado que lejos de aquí yo he anhelado.=Indignant
to the point far from here I have desired.

He Perdido Mi Paz

Es que mis pesadillas están atrás.= Is it that my nightmares are back.

He Perdido Mi Paz

Que no sea maliado jamas.= That I not be hurt again.

He Perdido Mi Paz

2/18/93

Para mi Laura.= For Me Laura

Hoy Yo Renaci.= Today I was reborn.

Ahora tengo la esperanza de presentar mi nueva danza.=Now
I have the hope of presenting the new dance.

Hoy Yo Renací

Las cosas mejoraron para mi.=Things have gotten better for me.

Vendrás en Abril tu una militar yo un civil= You will
come in April you a military and me a civilian.

Hoy Yo Renaci

Para que me hagas revivir.= So that you will revive me.

Hoy Yo Renací

Yo un civil tu una militar.= Me a civilian you a military.

Este amor no lo voy a soltar.= This love I'm not letting go.

Hoy Yo Renaci

2/18/93

Recuerdos Dulces.= Sweet Memories.

Viajando por mi país en mi ni~nes.= Travelling
my country as in my childhood.

Aventura fue la raíz de mi vejez.= Adventure was the root of my old age.

Recuerdos Dulces

Andando, Andando por coche,avión y tren.=
Going going by car,plane and train.

Orando,Orando A Dios gracias con mi amen.=
Praying,praying to GOD thanks with my amen.

Recuerdos Dulces

Con disputa o paz.= With dispute or peace.

Siempre adelante no atras.= Always forward never backward.

Recuerdos Dulces

2/19/93

Io Credo Che sia Caspita.=I Believe That What A Pity

Quando parliamo Io non capito di cui parliamo.=When
we speak I don't understand whom we speak.

Io credo che sia caspita.

Nessuno saprà perche.= Noone will know.

Io credo che sia caspita.

Oggi si e oggi no.= Today yes and today no.

Io credo che sia caspita.

Tutto il mondo parla cose cose.= All the world speak things things.

io credo che sia caspita.

Io non vuole mai tutti parliamo di questa.=I don't
want but everyone talks about this.

io credo che sia caspita.

Ma che situazione ha detto.= But what situation has said.

io credo che sia caspita.

Solo una parola comincia tutto.= Only a word starts everything.

io credo che sia caspita.

2/19/93

Ciebe Com O Céu = Free Like The Sky

Quero ser ciebe.= I want to be free.

Ciebe com o Céu pra onde eu nasceu.=I want to be
free like the sky to go to where I was born.

Pelo as nuvens.= By the clouds.

Ciebe com o céu este galego sonha por sua terra n~ae.= I want
to be free like the sky this Gallician dreams for his native land.

Cando era rapazinho.= when he was a boy.

Ciebe Com O Ceu.

Caminhando por caminho não como coelho pra um chão.=
Walking by the road not like a rabbit for a field.

Ciebe Com O Ceu

2/22/93

Brisa = Breeze

Tu tienes una bella sonrisa.= You have a beautiful smile.

Brisa

Se siente como un fria brisa.= It feels like a cold breeze.

Brisa

Solo vivo dia a dia.= I only live day to day.

Lo que mas quiero no se perdia.= I want more that is not lost.

Brisa

Me acompañaras siempre.= I am accompanied always.

Brisa

Te sentiré aún en la frente.= I shall feel even in the front.

Brisa.

2/22/93

Tiempo So~nalento= Sleepy Time

Tube sue~nos sin due~nos.= I had dreams without owners.

tiempo so~nalento

El duende tiene un individual que depende.= The
leprechaun has an individual that depends.

tiempo so~nalento

Quien mostrará el destino?.= Who has shown destiny?

tiempo so~nalento

De DIOS uno se guía en su camino.= Of GOD one must guide their path.

tiempo so~nalento

Por eso no me tormento.= For this I do not torment.

2/23/93

6 Semanas=6 Weeks.

Son 6 semanas mas para ser libre.=6 more weeks to be free.

Afuera de mi casa tocaré el timbre=Outside
my house I will press the doorbell.

6 Semanas

Espero ser un civil antes del mes de Abril.=I wait to
become a civilian before the month of April.

6 Semanas

Yo Quiera ir me con mi Luana= I want to go with my Luana.

6 Semanas

Para Bailar en la ciudad Gaditana.= To dance in the city of Cadiz.

6 Semanas

Estaré en España, se fuma tabaco y se Bebe Más sangría. =I shall be
in Spain, where they smoke tobacco, and they drink more sangria.

6 Semanas.

2/27/93

Las Horas= The Hours

Todos mis anhelos siempre con esos celos.= All my
wishes are always with those jealousies.

Todavía quiero estar en mi casa.=Even though
the hours I want to be in my house.

Entre mi raza lejos otra vez de que porque.= In between
my race far one more time of the what.

Vivo lleno de tristeza las horas porque se va mi belleza las horas.=It
is filled with sadness because my beauty is passing the hours.

3/27/93

Quiero Volver A Renascer= I want to be reborn.

Hay tanto en mi querer= There is so much in my wants.

Qué es lo que puedo hacer quiero volver a renascer.=
What is it that I can do is to be reborn.

Yo intente ser un soldado ahora soy un loco hospitalizado.= I
tried to become a soldier but now I'm crazy in the hospital.

Quiero volver a renacer

En el mes de Abril yo quiero revivir para ser un civil.= In the
month of April I want to revive to become a civilian.

Cuánto volver tiempo me espera el triunfo hago que me haga
feliz en que planta mi raiz.= I want to return to the time where
the triumph waits to make me happy like the plant of my root.

Quiero volver a renacer.

4/3/93

Rapazinho California.= Californian Boy.

Cando eu voltar a minha terrinha nae?.= When will I return to my native land?

Cando o rapazinho eu comia o sopa de faba.= When I was a boy I ate bean soup.

Acordou cando minha nae falava.= I remember when my mom would speak.

Eu estava com a laverca voando pelo ar.= I was with the lark flying through the air.

Andava pela chao pelo prado.= I was walking by the field and the meadow.

O rapazinho californiano comia batates frites com minha gunja.= The Californian boy ate fried potatoes with my indian licorice.

4/8/93

Confuso,Confuso Estoy.= Confused,Confused I Am

Mi corazon me dira a donde.= My heart will tell to where.

Voy sin razon me hiere al carbon. = I go without
reason it wounds me to carbon.

Esta situacion indecison.= This situation indecision.

Mi vida tiene otra vuelta despierta.=my life has another woken turn.

Tantas emociones sin las canciones.= So
many emotions without the songs.

Me veo desdichado endeudado.= I see myself disinherited and in debt.

Confuso Confuso estoy

Suicidio es mi solucion quizas sera cortoplazo.= Suicide
is my solution perhaps it will be short term.

Pero mi padre y abuela tendran un ataque al cardiaco.= But
my dad and grandmother will have a cardiac arrest.

O mi hermana perdera la criatura en el largo plazo.=
Or my sister will lose the babe in the long run.

Suicidio por esta razon no lo hago.=Suicide
for this reason I will not do it.

Confuso Confuso estoy me veo desdichado endeudado.=Confused
,Confused I am disinherited and in debt.

4/29/93

Ara Jo Vull.= Now I Want

Ara jo vull mevas donnes= Now I want my women.

Ara jo vull meua terra. = Now I want my land.

Les coses ara jo vull mes que. = The things I now want more than.

Ara jo vull meva casa. = I want my house.

les taules difficultates ara jo estoc lluny de meus amics et
amicas.= The tables are difficult now I am far from my friends.

Una vegada per el moment un llobaro i un anyel.=
One time for the moment a wolf and a lamb.

Tancats meva porta per el cami per anar a meua
ciutat totos aqui totas a aca. =Closed my door by the
road to walk to my city all here alll over here.

La nit et cort el jorn et llarg.= The night and the court the day is long.

Les paureles que sali de meua boca. = The
words of that come out of my mouth.

Jo strany a meus amistats.= I miss my friendships.

Jo penso hi les temps pasats quan jo te bes.=I think
of the times past when I would kiss you.

Vostedes volie de me perque jo et trist.= You
want of me because I am sad.

Cathascu tenem sua vida perque jo n'ho la meva.=Each
one of you has thier life because I don't have mine.

La meu dany me sentiu cru. = My damage makes me feel raw.

Me sentiu nu ara nit. =I feel naked now at night.

Ara jo vull .= Now I want.

4/29/93

Acolada De Amor=Accolade Of Love

Abaixo meu cor.= Below my heart.

Per un prat jo vist una bella donna anar.= by a
meadow I see a beautiful woman walk.

Hi tant de tant que jo la spere es dit si me vull a me.=There
is so much of that I wait it is said that I want for me.

Quan jo parle con aquiexa dona.= When I speaks to that woman.

Ela me deciu te pergunta algu de voste.= She
told me ask something of you.

De on eres es com nos coneixem?=Where are you from?

Que farem com esta avui ara.=What shall we do with today now.

Hi pocs moments fer el amor fins ara meu amor.
=There is few moments to make love ends now

06/12-13/09

Come Vuoi? = What Do You Want?

Come vuoi che il sole apparire?=What do
you want for the sun to appear?

Perché vai piovere?=Why is it going to rain?

Ma Ancora dopo non spergersi!=But still later not to be wasted.

Niente!=Nothing!

Tutto che io ho in mente.=Everything that I have in my mind.

Ma io vedo che il cielo blu.=But I see that the sky is blue.

Stai lassù.=It is on.

Molto semplice la natura.=Very simple nature.

Questo è come la scultura.=This is like the sculpture.

Ancora e il compleanno di mio nipote.=Still
and the birthday of my nephew.

Tutta la famiglia vieni cui.= All the family is coming here.

Per celebrare il seso aniversario di Nicola.= To
celebrate the session of Nicholas' birthday.

Gia uscire il sole allora è meglio.=Now comes
out the sun now and better.

Ma non gli fiori perche Nicola e un ragazzo.=But
not flowers because Nicholas is a boy.

06/12-13/09

Kedando En Kaza= Staying In House

Me e enfastyado de estar en bayita.= I am angry at being at home.

El enfastyamento no se me kita.= The anger does not leave me.

Ma sigo adelantre kon mis linguas estranyeras mi piyyutim.= I continue forward with my foreign languages and my torah poems.

La poezia se me kita del korason.= Poetry come from my heart.

Kuando tengo emosyon.=when I have emotion.

Ainde skrivia muchos poemas era kolay.=Even though I wrote many poems it was easy.

Agora no me kitan muncho ajay!= Now they don't come out much oh!

Ande estan mis piyut ke iskundyeron non rengrasyaron?=where are my torah poems that were hidden without gratitude.?

Entonses seguire kon lu ke kita de mi nefesh!=then follow with what I take from my soul!

Dimi lo ke keresh?=Tell me what you want?

Kuando vo ir afuera en bayita?=When will I go outside the house?

Ke agora se me faze galera!= That now it makes a jail!

El ayre baldayon me aspera.=The air heavy that awaits me.

Ke me komi una pera= That I ate a pear.

Sintiendo mi muzika.=Hearing my music.

Tambyen la del Afrika.=Also the one from Africa.

Munchas kosikas ke azer en kaza.=Many little things to do at home.

Kaji se me perye la fraza.=I almost lost the phrase.

Tengo dos perras i kuatro perrikos.= I have two dogs and foour puppies.

No kero ulbidar todo komo los asnikos era kolay.=No I don't want to forget like if they were little mules like that was easy.

E yir al kal para vyernes.=And go to the synagogue for Friday.

Fazer para finir dospues.= To do to finish later.

Ma no todo al roves.=but not everything backwards.

Dizin ke so ladino.= They say I am a Sephardic speaker.

Ma no se lo ke tengo en tino?=I don't know what I have in mind.

Kuando tengo emosyon.=When I have emotion.

Ainde skrivia munchos poemas era kolay.=Even
though I wrote many poems it was easy.

Agora no me kitan muncho ajay!=Now they don't take much ah!

Ainde estan mis piyut Ke se iskunderyon non rengrasyaron.= Even
though there are my torah poems that were hidden without thanking.

11/03/09

Oceano=Ocean

Tus alrededores de árboles y palmeras,Océano de
San Diego,California es en ti que se sonia. en cuanto
camino adentro como quiera=To your sides of trees and
Palms Ocean of San Diego,California it is you in which
we dream right by the road inside when I want.

Cuando camino por sus playas me siento calmado en paz con
las hojas y palmas en lo verde.=When I walk by your beaches
I feel calm in peace with the leaves and palms in green.

Me digo si no quiero un sas con agua todo se desprendre.=I
tell myself if I do a blow with water everything runs out.

Veo la belleza de tu naturaleza, tus pequeñas piedras a la diestra.=I
see the beauty of your nature,your small pebbles to the left.

Las aves,ardillas y focas me hacen pensar en la izquierda.= The
birds,squirrels and sea lions make me think on the left.

O oceano a ti no te vuelven loca veo tus chicas islas ancladas
de animales.= The ocean to you they do not return they
drive you crazy in your small islets sunken with animals.

Ya vi me sereno en tus verde rocas esas son las
focas y las aves.=I am seen serene in your green
rocks; these are the sea lions and birds.

La arena entre mis pies en la hondura puedo ver ballenas.=
The sand between my legs in your depths I can see whales.

Aun no puedo hallar al ciempiés estas son felices y plenas.=Even
though I can't find centipedes which are happy and full.

Ver tus hierbas y zacate una ave marítima sobre un tejado.=See
your green herbs and grass like a seabird over a roof.

La verdor y frescura tus partes jamás se cambie mi hado.=The
green and freshness of your parts never change like your destiny.

La alga marina en tus colinas me fascinan disfrutar el océano
te daré la mano.=The marine seaweed in your hills fascinate
me enjoying the ocean. I will give you the hand.

Ver todo tu esplendor de tus almejas preciosas sin
que haya una choza.=To see all of the splendor of your
precious clams without there being a hut.

11/17/09

Horton Plaza

Today I went in a convoy of 7 today to Horton Plaza without my raza.

I spent it eating Indian food that I shared with Rudy.

It was a pleasure to be followed as a leader while I saw a cutey.

We went to Sam Goody where Noelle bought a music C'd.

I enjoyed the music so pretty.

There were many people shopping.

I could just imagine Mary Poppins.

Lilia bought cookies while we ate lunch.

She was following a hunch .

I did not buy anything except food, however it was good.

There were so many stores I could not count the scores.

11/17/09

Sinagoga = Synagogue

Yo vo ala sinagoga ke yamo esnoga en chabbat.= I go to
the synagogue that I call temple on the Sabbath.

Dezde leshos de Rabat.= From afar of Rabat.

Vo a San Diego a Ohr Shalom en Chabbat.= I go
to San Diego to Ohr Shalom in Sabbath.

Ma a Tiferet Israel en Alhad a San Carlos.= But
to Tiferet Israel in Sunda to San Carlos.

Para ambezar djudezmo en kal diya de alhad.=To
learn Judiasm in the day of Sunday.

Primo el kulto a la kehila diya de chabbat.= First the
worship to the house of God day of Friday.

Todos d'estos nomvres de sinagoga.= All
these names for the synagogue.

Yo me vo el fin de la semana ala snoga.=I
go to the weekend to the schul.

Agora vo ser kontente stando kon mi djente.=Now
I go happy with my people.

Spiritualamente vo al templo ansi yo me asendo la neshama
=Spiritually I go to the temple also I light my soul.

Komo estar en kaza de la flama la kamareta de flama.=Like
being in the house of flame the bedroom of flame.

11/18/2009

El Gato de Visiones=The Cat Of Visions

Este gato tiene muchos nombres.=This cat has many names.

Que todos le llamamos en Visiones.=We all call him in Visions.

Unos le dicen Henry,yo le digo Pardo El Varón o
Spots The Tom Cat.=Some call him Henry,I call
him the dark male or Spots The Tom Cat.

No se como le llaman los demás?Patches?=I don't
know what others call him?Patches?

Este gato tiene genio, es muy cariñoso pero no ranoso!=This
cat has genius and is very endearing but not rancid!

Todos lo abrazamos o levantamos.=We all hug or pick him up.

Todos nosotros queremos al gato mejor que un
pato.= We all love the cat better than a duck.

Siempre lo miramos al rato.= We always see him once in a while.

Va y viene pero no nos retiene.= He comes
and goes but does not retain.

El es blanco pero pardo oscuro, está gordo y grande.=
He is white but pitch dark,he is big and fat.'

Estará con nosotros hasta que Dios mande.= He
will be with us that God will determine.

Es definitivamente curioso amorós Henry.=
It's Definitely curious loving Henry.

11/18/09

Rocha Verde =Green Rock

Umas rochas verdes perto do mar. = Some green rocks next to the sea.

Sempre andamos pra falar.= We are walking to talk.

A natureza que beleza.= To nature what a beauty.

À beira mar sinto a pintar o pinto.=To the
edge of the sea to paint or painting.

Quem pode me dizer que faço pra valer ?=Who
can say I said I can do to be worthy.

Muitas coisas lindas que vejo ainda.=Many things I can still see.

Rocha verde juntas as rochas da praia e como eu que saia!=Green
rock together with rocks of the beach and how I can go out!

Vejo todo bonito que tem a natureza pra mim é uma fortaleza.=
Everything beautiful that has nature for me and a fortress.

Belos horizontes do verdor uma força com ardor.=Beautiful
horizons of green with a force of spirit.

Temos fervor da vida pelo mar e natureza.=We
have fervour of life by the sea and nature.

Somos gente com amor, todos sem dor.=We
people love all without pain.

12/07/09

Lluvia=Rain

Porque tuvo que caer la lluvia?=Why did the rain have to fall?

Por qué la tierra estaba sucia?=For what reason the land was dirty?

Para que la tierra seca sedienta beba el agua.=For
the land is dry and thirsty to drink water.

Desde Chihuahua hasta Managua.=From Chihuahua to Managua.

Yo me empape de mojarme.=I soaked myself wet.

Cansado no puedo arrodillarme.=Tired I could not kneel.

Todos aquí adentro.cada quien en su centro.=Everyone
here inside each one in their midst.

No hay mucho que hacer mas uno tiene que comprender.=There
is not a lot to do but one has to understand.

Yo sé que es necesario pero no quiero ser voluntario.=I
know it is necessary but I want to volunteer.

Tampoco que llueva diario.=Nieither for it to rain daily.

Todavía hay mucho que se pueda hacer adentro.=There
is still much that can be done inside.

Para que encuentre me contento.=So that I can find myself content.

El si y no el otro espectro.= The yes and no of the other spectrum.

Todos recogidos adentro yo no lo lamento.=All picked up inside I don't cry.

Es un día como tal. nos vino la lluvia para cada cual.=It is
a day as such.It came to us rain for each one of us.

Yo extraño un dia con sol sin jugar beisbol.=I miss
a day in the sun without playing baseball.

Pero para mi la lluvia lo arruino todo.Yo me moje de todo modo.=But
for me the rain ruined everything.I got wet no matter what.

Quisiera que cesara para que no haya más lluvia.=I
wanted it to cease for no more rain

12/07/09

Falling Leaves

I see the falling leaves fall from the trees.

It is a sign of winter.

They are leaves not splinters.

Gray,white clouds remind me of burial shrouds.

The beginning and the end of life cycles.

The foliage of the trees changes by the hour.

The colors go from green to sweet and sour.

Many people driving must slow down or
else they run on shallow ground.

The leaves falling like a merry go round.

The trees swaying back and forth with the wind running.

It's nature's way of showing cunning.

Falling leaves without pet leaves.

If they rake them.

When It stops raining the sun will bake them.

The floors of the earth are soaked with leaves.

As I walked I hoed and heaved.

Falling leaves are in the air with winter time to spare.

When the leaves fall they die it makes them want to sigh.

To me it is nature's cry.

12/07/09

Floresika Blanka De Hanuka=The little White Flower Of Chanukah

La floresika blanka i mavi komo los kolores de hanuka.=The little white and blue like the colors of Chanukah.

Ya guelo los dulses golores sin dizir charuka=I smell the candies sweet smells without saying a sandal.

Kantika de mi nona.=Little song by my grandmother.

Eya no se yamo Karmona.=She is not called Carmona.

Agora asendemos las kandelas.=We turn on the Candles.

Ansi ke keremos ver las velas.= Like this we want to see the sails.

Todos endjuntikos vamos a baylar i kantar.=Everyone together to dance and sing.

las kansiones mos emosyonan.=The songs will fill us with emotion.

Las kantikas mos aboltan.=The songs make us return.

Shiru,Shira hadash.= Song ,Sing a new.

Ande vamos,ande stas?=Where to or where we are?

Kontentes kon alegriyas de la hanukia.=Content with joys of Menorah.

Todos mozotros estamos komiendo birmuelos kon muestros aguelos.=We all are eating fritters with our grandparents.

Ande vaj estas nochadas de hanuka djugar las kartikas sin dezir shaka.=Where are you going this nights of Chanukah play the cards without saying jokes.

Munchas kumidas savrosas y los gateaus delizyosos.=Many savory foods and delicious cakes.

Beviendo Chikolata i komiendo bonbones.=Drinking hot chocolate and eating bonbons.

Lo bueno no es agristda kon peshe kon limones.=The good isn't fish with mayonaisse with lemons.

Mos ponemos las bragas.= We put on our breeches.

Kon las paras es el diya de paga.=With the money it is payday.

Hanuka,hanuka ay ke baylar las charukas.=Chanukah,Chanukah lets you dance with slippers.

Kantaremos larala larala.=We will sing larala larala.

Al DIO Alto munchas grasyas.=To GOD thank you much.

Bendicho las famiya Maccabiah.=Blessed be the Maccabee Family.

Mos libraron de los Gregos.=They freed us of the Greeks.

Sin Temermos.= Without us fearing.

Agora tenemos hanuka.=Now we have Chanukah.

12/17/09

Ke Ago Agora?=What Do I Do Now?

Agor no se ke fazer.=Now I don't know what to do.

Hanuka se kita el ultimo diya.=Chanukah is over the last day.

Amanyana ya no segimos la karavana.=Tomorrow
we don't follow the caravan.

Las luezikas ya no asendidas.=The lights no longer lit.

sin tener las hanukias pedridas.=Without having the menorahs lost.

Vyernes 18 las ultimas kandelas asendidas.=Friday
18th the last candles are lit.

Ya no tengo muzika djudiya espesyala.=I
don't have special Jewish Music.

Esto kon triztura yine de amrgura .=I am sad and bitter.

Ya no ay hanuka.= There is no more Chanukah.

Asta el anyo vinien.=Till the coming year.

Kreigo ke estare byen.=I believeI will be okay.

Asperando en asender las hanukias para el proksymo anyo.=
I am waiting to light the menorahs for next year.

Nadika mas tengo el plazer de lo ke vo azer.=Nothing
of the pleasurable than that I will do.

12/21/09

Vida=Life

Esta vida llena de sorpresa.=This life is full of surprises.

Hace que inventa en la cabeza.=To invent in the head.

Quiero vivir feliz en mi país.=I want to live happily in my country.

Un año tuve mi lugar.=A year that I had my own place.

Ahora yo no puedo estar!=Now I can not be there!

Vida porque no me despidas.=Life because you don't say goodbye.

Tiempo del arco iris me toco.= Time of the rainbow touched me.

Todos los colores con los sinsabores.=All the
colors without the bitterness.

El color negro esta en mi vida.=The color black is in my life.

Porque no tengo es movida.=Because I don't have is moved.

Espero renacer para volver.=I wait to be reborn to return.

Hacer lo mismo de antes.=To do the same as before.

Catrin y cantante.=Well dressed and a singer.

Un revés otra vez.=A blow and another time.

Cuando acabara esta mala vibra.=When will this bad vibe finish or stop.

Pienso que pierdo la fibra=I think that I lose the fiber.

Que hare para recapacitar.=What shall I do to recapacitate?

Yo ya no puedo dar.=I can not give anymore.

Vivo de dia a dia.=I live day to day.

Sin las maravillas=Without the marvells.

Luchando por mi bien=Fighting for my good.

Al mismo tiempo.= At the same time.

Tengo que madurar.=I must mature.

Necesito paciencia.=I need patience.

Pedirle a DIOS clemencia.=Ask GOD for mercy.

Quedar bien en su presencia.=To be good in his presence.

Vida detestda.=Hateful life.

Donde esta mi vara.=Where is my stick.

Acaso vales nada!=Are you worth nothing!

12/21/09

Carolling

I believe in the holiday cheer spreading joy in a day clear.

I love carolling for young and old. Those that love to sing are bold.

Hearing their timbre a capella gets you going fella.

From clubhouses to crisis centers to hospitals.

We go carolling bringing hope to those that don't have it.

To see them, clapping,singing and dancing brings their spirits up.

Singing a new song to the lord on top.

It makes me happy to come as a group.

Filling every last drop to scoop after I have had my soup.

With Christmas,Hanukkah,Kwanzaa,Eid ul fitr and New Years.

I won't have to sing the blues.

I love to go carolling and bring a smile to their face.

So they can feel the holiday trail.

Eggnog, hot apple cider and hot chocolate to spare in Santa's Lair.

You see I'm cool, not square.

Seeing the moon shine with mistletoe and twine.

Happy holidays a carolling.

12/21/09

Quero=I Want

Eu quero um feliz natal e próspero ano novo.=I want
a Merry Christmas and Happy New Year.

Pra você e tudo mundo.=For you and everyone in the world.

A DEUS eu pedi tudo isso.=To GOD I ask that.

Quero uma mulher pra casar.=I want a woman to marry.

Ninguém sabe o que quero mais.=Nobody knows what I want more.

Também filhos da nova famílha.=Also children from a new family.

Um autocarro e a casa.=A car and a house.

Estar contente com a vida.=To be happy with life.

De repente resplendente.=All of a sudden resplendent.

O arco com as cores de beijar as lindas flores.=the
rainbow of colors to kiss the beautiful flowers.

O perfume linda aroma myrta de goma.=A sweet
aroma of perfume of resin of myrtle.

Eu Quero puro que a você eu adouro=I want
pure for you that I adore you.

01/25/10

Eu Estou Contento=I Am Content

Eu estou contente com meu apartamento e ele não
é grande pra mim.=I am content with my apartment
and elegant as well as extremely big for me.

Tudo que tenho está em malas excepto umas
coisas não balas.=Everything that I have is in
suitcases accept the things not bullets.

Quero morar muitos anos em minha morada como cantando uma
balada.=I want to live many years in my abode with me singing a ballad.

Eu quero ter minha fada.=I want to have my fairy godmother.

Trocar meu fado pra bem.=I want to change my destiny for good.

Dizer amém eu estou contente.=I say amen I am content.

Não tenho um lamento.=I don't have a lament.

Tudo vai assim pra mim.=Everything goes like this for me.

01/25/10

Many Hours

I waited many hours so bored I counted flowers.

The days seemed like hours that I made a face like scours.

I waited a long time for my apartment.

So much stuff to put in the compartment.

No furniture was my lament.

Friends brought some for development.

Many hours in the showers.

Keeping busy and clean trying to lose weight and be lean,

Many hours that I did not smell the flowers.

01/25/10

Mi Apartamento=My Apartment

Mi apartamento no tyene lamento.= My apartment has no lament.

Esto kontente estar sin la djente.= I am content without the people.

aleskuras sin agruras.=Dark without heartburn.

Todo klaro kon mamparo.= Everything clear with backup.

Todo el diya esto de maraviya.=all day it's of marvels.

Felis komo el ladino halis.= Happy like JudeoSpanish pure.

Esto de fyesta kon la alegrika.=I am celebrating with joy.

Ke tyene mi luguar kitadika.= Who has a place taken.

La alegriya de mi shara.=Happiness of my forest?

A kapara.=Forgiveness of sins offerings.

Munchos anyos i mas kero en mi luguar.= Many
years and more I want in my place.

Para kuzir i fadar.=To sow and female naming ceremony.

Dospues dar kidushin.=Later solemly marriage.

Sin malshin.=Without slander.

Agora vo estar sin el kadar.=Now I will be without up to.

01/25/10

Mi lugarcito=My Place

Tengo mi lugarcito por un ratito.=I have a place for a while.

No se cuando yo me repito.=I don't know when I repeat myself.

Quiero vivir allí muchos años.=I want to live there for many years.

Para no perder escanos.= To not lose scans.

De la noche al día se me va la maravilla.=From
night to day to the marvel.

Aún estoy contento con mi apartamento.=Even
though I am content with my apartment.

Ahora ya no hay lamentos.=Now there are no more laments.

Porque me quedo tranquilo, soy gordo y quiero perder el
quilo.=Because I am tranquil,I'm fat and want to lose weight.

Como a gusto sin ver el busto.=I eat comfortably without the bust.

Si es la mujer guapa no me asusto.=Yes she is a
good looking woman I am not scared.

Estoy de repente con buena mente.=I am with
you repeatedly with a good mind.

Yo ya no soy ausente.=I am not absent.

Mi lugarcito como si fuera papacito.= My place is like I was daddy O.

01/25/10

Je Veux Être Heureux En Mon Propre Appartement.=I Want To Happy In My Own Apartment.

Chante une chanson de joie et n'en déplorez=. Sing a song of joy and no lament.,

Me disent une histoire des différends de survie de la vie de Ysmael's.=Tell me a story of Ysmael's life surviving strife.

Avant que soit son appartement qu' I n'était pas vivant.=Before his apartment he was not alive.

Pour ceci est ce qu'il tache.=For this is what he strives.

L'indépendance n'est pas venue bon marché'.=Independance did not come cheap.

Particulièrement pleurant pour lui sur un tas.=Especially crying for it on a heap.

Le prix de la liberté était si raide.=The price of freedom was so steep.

Mais aucun se coucher au flauge.=but no lving down to creep.

Libérez remercient enfin librement la puissance de Dieu=Free at last free at last thank God almighty I'm free at last.

01/25/10

Per Sempre.=Forever

Per sempre in un giorno lo preso per ottenere il mio
posto.= forever in a day it took me to get my place.

Sono un uomo non mettero il merletto.=I am a man will not put lace.

Felice e L'uomo che ha il suo proprio castello.=Happy
is the man that has his own castle.

Piu lotta nient'altro non fastidi.=No more fights, no more hassles.

Ho speso più parte interna di tempo che non cerca una
fidanzata.I spent more time inside not looking for a bride.

Prendendo a cura del commercio nessuno al
viluppo=Taking care of business no one to mess.

Giornalieri viventi come esso erano miei
durano.=Living everyday like it was my last.

Completamente rompendosi con il mio
passato.=Totally breaking with my past.

02/08/10

Kero Bivir=I Want To Live

Kero bivir para azer Santo.=I want to live to become holy.

Agora ke vo kon mi manto.= Now I go with my blanket.

Munchas vezes vo sekularo.=Many times I go secular.

Al DIO ALTO=To GOD the most high.

Le do i rengrasyo.= I give and appreciate.

Por todas mis berachot.= For all my blessings.

Soltanto una palavrika.=Just one word.

El me libero de mi ermanika i konyado..=He delivered
me from my little sister and brother in law.

Agora bivo en National City.=Now I live in National City.

Sivdad ande yo engrandesi.= City where I grew up.

Por esto digo mersi.= For this reason I say thanks.

No ay nadika komo mi etaj=There is nothing like my apartment.

Para ke veas los ke konoskaj.=That you may see and know.

Mis mushos no se pyedren el tefila.=My lips don't lose the prayer.

Esto agrdesido de la bida.=I am grateful for life.

Munchas oras de saar i ansyedad pasi.=Many
times of bitterness and anxiety.

Yo mezmo me kontente i emosyoni.=I gladden
myself and got emotional.

Yo no me pedri.= I am not lost.

No ay nada ke yo me di,=There is nothings.

Amen baruch hashem amen.=Amen blessed be GOD amen.

Ninguno saviya loke me afitava.=Noone
knew what was happening to me.

Bendicho el Dio tengo morada.= Blessed be GOD that I have an abode.

Yo puedo meldar i eskrivir i ambezar.=I can read, write and learn.

En la pas.=In peace.

Nunka kero yo yorar.=I never want to cry.

Ni pasar momentos aravyar.= Nor pass moments of rage.

Felis i kontente kero estar.=Happy and content I want to be.

EL DIO bendiko seya syempre.= Blessed be GOD always.

02/08/10

Hoy la luz=Today The light

Hoy estoy disfrutando la luz del dia.=I am enjoying the light of day.

Yo sentado en mi silla.=Seating in my seat.

No mas para mi la vilchia.= No more of the suffering for me.

Darle gracias por mi pan de cada dia.=I give
him thanks for my daily bread.

A DIOS MEDIANTE.=GOD be willing.

Ya soy un cantante.= I am a s nger.

Hay que ir adelante.=Lets go forward.

Hoy vi la luz sin comer coouscous de Marruecos..=Today I had an
epiphany that I saw the light without eating couscous of Morocco.

Mi vida la vivo plena muy llena.=My life I live it full and complete.

Tengo muchas classes.=I have a lot of classes.

Yo i Maria hicimos las pases.=Me and Mary made peace.

Espero que Rhonda me perdone.=I hope Rhonda will forgive me.

Hasta que venga si se lo pone en perdonar.W=Till
she comes to be in a mood to forgive.

Estaré listo para cantar.=I will be ready to sing.

Hoy vi la luz sin decir Jesus.=today I saw the light without saying Jesus.

02/08/10

life

My life is better than ever today.

Hey hey hey

I found my way.

What can I say?

I'm home again to stay at visions.

No more revisions.

Let's rocknroll for I'm on the dole.

Let me sing with joy because poetry is my old toy.

I'm a man not a boy.

Who's still drinking soy.

Life is good for I have my own place.

Now I can save face with some money to spare.

Sing my poetry I dare from my soul comes my cares.

02/08/10

Feliz Da Vida=Happy of life

Feliz da vida eu vou sem saída.=Happy of life I go without an exit.

Entrada quero para minha vida.= Entry I want for my life.

Não sou infeliz demais.=I am not unhappy anymore.

Meus estudos satisfaz.=My studies satisfied.

Mais que nada, já voltei às visões.=More than anything I returned to visions. Aprendindo meus licoes.=I am learning my lessons.

Não, mais quero dizer adeus.=No more I want to say goodbye.

Ninguém sabia que eu voltaria .=Noone knew I would return.

Eu volto pra sempre só quero Deus.=I return forever that GOD wants.

Minhas emoções estavam florescendo.=My emotions were flourishing.

Porque eu sou livre para renascer.= I am free to be born.

Tudo estou bom pra ver.=Everything is good to see.

Eu posso estudar,ler e aprender.=I can study ,read and learn.

Todo issto e assim.=Everytning is is like this.

Climbing The Walls

It seems deep down I am climbing the walls. I keep myself from hitting the stalls. I can't stand Covid-19 lockdown from town. I want my freedom to roam and do things. I can't be with my friends. Everyone everywhere don't you dare is not.

02/08/10

Miracle

Chaque jour pour moi est un miracle.=Every day for me is a miracle.

Je n'ai jamais pensé que je respirais librement encore à San Diego.=I never thought I could breathe free again in San Diego.

Dieu a répondu à mes prières et m'a donné un appartement pour vivre dedans.=GOD answered my prayers and gave me an apartment to live in.

Pour étudier,me reposer et écrire de la poésie. To study,sit and write poetry.

Apprenez les langues libres comme l'air.=Learn my languages free as the air.

Je compte mes bénédictions nuit et jour.=I count my blessings night and day.

je trouve des solutions pour ces problèmes dans la raison.=I find solutions for my problems within reason.

L'indépendance est ma saison.=Independnce is my season.

Laissez-moi sentir la qualité venir à ma rencontre.=Let me feel the goodness come my way.

Des visions je suis ici pour rester.=Vision's I'm here to stay.

Pas plus se vautrant dans la boue.=No more wallowing in the mud.

Je n'ai pas obtenu mon endroit parlé par HUD.=I did not get my place by HUD.

Demain pour moi est un autre beau jour.=tomorrow for me is another good day.Les choses semblent balancer ma maniere.=Things seem to swing my way..

02/08/10

Wild Poetry.=Poesia Salvaggia

Sometimes I am wild with abandon with my poetry.=A volte
sono selvaggio con abbandono con la mia poesia.

It is balanced with asymmetry.= E equilibrata con assimetria.

The melodies that come out..=le melodie que uscite

From a wellspring they sproutt.=Da un sorgente germogliano.

It is my happiness blossoming.=Suo mio sbocciare di felicità.

I'm humming and humming.=Sono ronzante e ronzante.

It's life all over again.=E vita ancora una volta.

Now you know where I'm in.=Ora sapere cove sono dentro.

The music flows with no blows of the lungs.=La
musica scorre senza colpi dei polmoni.

This is spun.=Questo racconto è filato.

No more living life on the run.=Non più vita vivente sul funzionamento.

Now I can have fun .=Ora posso divertirmi.

The true Ysmael has been freed.=Il Ysmael Vero è stato liberato.

bEfore I would bleed.=Prima che sanguina

2/22/10

La Comida Mejicana.=Mexican Food

Quiero mi comida fresquecita y calientita pero no en la mano.= I want my food fresh and hot but not in the hand.

Comida variada y adecuada bajo el manzano.= Varied and adequate food under the apple tree.

Tan sabrosa que me chupo los dedos en dia de Verano.=So delicious that its finger linking good in a summer day.

Unos tacos,una quesadilla,mulas y sopes no mas me falto un poco de rompope..=Some tacos,a quesadilla,mulas and sopes no more missing just a little of Vajnilla rum,

Todas las delicias Mejicanas comiendo juntos en una Caravana vamonos recio vamonos a Tijuana.=All the Mexican delicacies eating together in a a caravan lets go full speed lets go to Tijuana.

Me pondre gordo de tanta Jactancia pero no me quiero enfermar del rancia quien sabe como se come en Francia.=I will get fat from all this boastfullness but I don't want to get sick from the rancid do you know how they eat in France.

Mas para mi no sea otra andancia .=More so that for me it will not be another sickness.

Hay que poner un altar ala cocina Mejicana Llamarle al restauran Tia Juana.=Lets put an altar to the Mexican Kitchen lets call the restaurant Aunt Jane.

Nada mas ponerle flan y llamar a Juan.= No more put flan and call to John.

Llamandole a million to one.=Calling it a million to Juan.

Una ranchera pasando las chelas sin habanera aun que no Quiera=A farm woman passing the beers without hot sauce even though I don't want.

La comida Mejicana no se me hace extrana la amo sobre todas las otras.the Mexican food is not strange I love it above all the others.

Como el caballo con su potra.=LIke the horse with its mare.

Conquistando fronteras hasta la riviera en la lejana
Costa Azul Francesa.=Conquering borders even
the Cote D'Azure of Frances Blue Coast.

No hay quien te compare entre los latino Americanos nada
que se hagalo haces en vano.=There is no comparison
between the latin Amercans nothing that is done in vain.

02/22/10

Capoeira

Capoeira danca que foi dos escravos.=A dance that was of slaves.

Tao brava como os cravos.=Very sharp like nails.

Bateam duro os bracos pra que que eu faco.=they
hit hard with their arms for that is what I do.

Tudo longe meus lacos.=It is far my ties.

Falamdo de mim e Antonio Carlos Jobim.= Speaking of me and Jobim.

Minha inglueca Brasileira eu ver uma palmeira do Brazil.=With
my brazilian influence I see a palm of BRazil.

Em mes do Abrill.=In the month of april.

Musica doce eu levo com mim o ritmo fortes.=SWeet
music I take with me the strong rhythms.

Capoeira da braisleira sem mortes.=The dance without deaths.

Bailando seu corpo que cortes.= Dancing their body cuts.

Tao fermosa mulher que te quero dizer coracao..=So
beautiful that wants to say heart.

02/22/10

Kibrites=Matches

Kibrites paras los sigaros ke afumar ya los diyas pasados.=Matches
for the cigarettes to smoke for days passed.

Agora es defendido afumar en publiko ni se auzan
los kibrites para el forno.=Now its prohibited to
smoke in public nor used in lighting the oven.

Munchos momentos estuvimos a fumando nargile.=Many
moments we smoked a water pipe.

Komo moztros vijitimos el desfile.=like we visited the parade.

Ya mos paso todo lo de muestra dor.=Everything
of our generation passec.

Es komo el mor del Bosfor.=Its like the love of the Bosphorus.

Kito el afumar sigaros aki en los estados unidos no mos
es de agrado.=I took away the smoking cigarettes here
in the United States. It is not pleasing for us.

En l'Amerika todo troka sin parar todo medido de karar.=In AMerika
everything changes without stopping everything measured by habit.

Las kozas de mozotros se desparesen.=OUr things disappear.

Komo si se efasan lo muestro esto me inche de triztura i hazinura.=Like
they erase our things it fills me with sadness and sickness.

Adio kibrites Ayde vate vites.=Goodbye matches beat it.

02/22/10

Today Is Special

today is special for me.

Its my birthday hey hey hey

I have no birthday cake to make.

No balloons for me to croon.

I wish I was born with a silverspoon.

Money and more money would make me happy.

So make it snappy.

where all the party people forget the church steeple.

Give me my wish come true.

O GOD you know what to do.

I'm a man not a shrew nor am I a bee with the dew.

02/22/10

Quando Biancha=When White

Quando Io Parlo un po di parole.=when I speak a few words.

Dove stai il mio amore.=Where is my love.

Come Io innamorato.= Like my boyfriend.

Il cuore ha chiamato.= The heart has called.

Bichiami ?bichiami? = What are you called? What are you called?

Dove Biancha la piccioli?=Where is White the small one?

Cara Cara Carina Bambina !=Dear dear Darling baby!

Che non si chiama Gina.=That is not called Jane.

Te vuoi dare un bacio sulla testa e un abbraccio.=I
want to give you a kiss with a hug.

Ti baci con il mio corpo.= I kiss you with my body.

Dopo faremo l'amore.=Later we make love.

Il mio cuor dice dove mi amor?=Where is my love?

Biancha non ti vedo mai!=White I don't see you again.!

Perche tu me lasse ai?=Why do you leave there?

02/22/10

Mon Coeur=My Heart

Ou est il mon cœur que j'ai perdu.=Where is my heart that I have lost.

Laissezmoi silvous plait quest ce que je
fais?=Leave me please what shall I do?

Un projet d'amour lire un livre d'une histoire.=A
project of love, read a historical book.

D'u Georgette qui a ver beaucoup des petite
amis.=Of Georgette that saw many lovers.

Elle se sent très jolis pasque fais trop de sexe la sensualite reignee'.=She
feels very happy for doing too much of the sex the sensual Queen.

Je dit la cite' de Montreal et du Georgette.=I say
the city of Montreal and of Georgette.

Mon coeur estil dan Montreal,Quebec.=My
heart is in Montreal,Quebec.

02/22/10

Beneath the Stars

Beneath the stars I watched the island on SeaWorld drive.

Across from me near the park it was beautiful despite the dark.

So peaceful and cold I did not want to leave yet bold .

Me and my friend walked on the grass because
there were many runners so I passed.

I enjoyed the crisp night air. It was so cold it lifted my hair.

I was feeling calm enjoying the night so calm, peaceful.

03/09/10

Today

Today I did not want to stay.

At home going crazy I start to stray.

I wanted to stay, I thought I might.

Keeping the madness at bay.

Staying busy is my only antidote.

The routine schedule keeps me afloat.

I don't want to rock the boat.

Today I had to get away from Visions .

I walked and took the bus.

Homeward bound in a fuss.

Cold day windy I will call it mindy.

I need release for my troubles to cease like ironing pants with a crease.

04/12/10

Una Redoma=A Bottle

Yo no kero el raki merkar si no Dr Pepper bever.=I
don't want to buy anise liqueur but Dr.Pepper.

Una delisya para mi bever Dr.Pepper.=A delicacy to drink Dr.Pepper.

Munchas vezes gratos pasi bevyendo Dr.Pepper.=Many
a pleasant times drinking Dr.Pepper.

Yo ainda ke engrandesi kon koka kola me plazio
muncho mas Dr.Pepper.=Even though I grew up with
Coca Cola, Dr Pepper pleased me more.

El kave kon dulsor Turko no lu kero mas sol tanto el chay
kayente.=Coffee with Turkish sweets I don't want anymore but hot tea.

Tomar i kumer boyikos i miyo Dr.Pepper.= Take
and eat pastries and my Dr.Pepper.

Agora so kontente kon mi redoma de Dr. Pepper es mas
savrozo ke la koka.=Now I am content with my bottle
of Dr.Pepper.it is more delicious than coke.

04/12/10

A Day Without Pets

I don't have pets in my house, not even a pubic louse.

I have a cleaner apartment.

No smells or hairs to worry about.

Its spicnspan my man an immaculate home to enjoy for the day.

NO animals greet me or grawl at prowlers.

I love where I live without pets.

A day without Pets I am profound without a dog.

To hound me as I leave or come home.

04/12/10

La Fruta Prohibida=The Forbidden Fruit.

Yo quiero comer lychee pero no está en la 99 más Ranch 88.=I want to eat lychee but it is not in the 99 but Ranch 88.

La longan no ha vuelto el rambután no es suelto.=The longan has not returned and the rambutan is not loose.

las frutas orientales tienen un sabor diferentes.=Orientals fruits have a different flavor.

Me gustan cuando están presentes los manjares exquisitos.=I like that ambrosia is exquisite when they are present.

No causan vómito son deliciosas cuando en jalea..=They don't cause vomit when they are delicious when in jam.

Pero ahora quieren que se escasee en la vida ha de todo.=but now they want what is scarce in life there is a little bit of everything.

Ya no tienen estas frutas ahora ni modo.=Now we don't have these fruits anymore.

Quisiera más fruto tropical pero más bien oiriental.=I want more tropical fruit but oriental.

04/12/10

Segunda Feira= Monday

Neste dia não foi movido e como foi esclarecido.=
This day was not moved like it was cleared.

Onde esta a gente do Clube Visoes.= Where
are the people of Visions Club.

Tudos sentados não fazendo nada ninguém pra fazer grupos
do dia e com sangue frio.=Everyone seated not doing nothing
noone for making groups of the day and the cold blood.

Neste dia lento não mais corpulento.=this
day slow it was not corpulent.

Meu corpo esperando na classe de música.=My
body waiting for the music class.

Eu quero sentir as vibrações da bateria.=I want
to hear the vibrations of the drums.

Olhar minhas poesias o clube e uma alma abatida neste dia.=I want to
show my poetry to the club and my soul has not abated to this day.

04/12/10

Dove Sta Musica = Where Is The Music

Where is the music that pleases me.=Where
is the music that pleases me.

I want peace. = I want peace.

Walking the street.=walking the street.

That no one sees the fairy that doesn't carry a sword.

All of life is lived simple. = All of life is lived simple.

I'm a little happy for I lack nothing.

I have friends,family, Visions Club ,social worker and a doctor.

I have a lot of books,cassettes and compact discs in the house.

There is not a single day I lack compassion.

Always for the beautiful vibrations.

Every Monday of the week a class of Music.

04/12/10

Retrouver Le Devine= Find The Divine

Help me find the divine=Aider me trouve le devine.

For it's a sense that is lost to most.=Pour
son un sens qui est perdu a plus.

It's like a spiritual host.= Son comment un hôte spirituel.

I need the spiritual in my life.=J'ai besoin du spirituel dans ma vie.

Since organized religion has failed me.=Puisque
la religion organisée' m'a échoué.

I wish they would keep politics out of it.=Je
souhaite qu'ils gardent la politique de lui.

That they would stop hurting me.=Qu'ils m'arreteraient de blesser.

Retriever le devine

My life has inner peace with spirituality.=Ma vie
a la paix intérieure avec la spiritualité.

To worship alone is a technicliaty.=Pour
adorer seul est un détail technique.

Help me find the goodness in life.=Aide me trouve la bonté dans la vie.

04/15/10

San Diego Trolley

You are a cacophony of voices.

All colors,nationalities and humanity.

You are the red Jewel that beckons back and forth.

The hustle and bustle that is the San Diego Trolley.

04/16/10

On The Bus 41

It's a short ride to the VA it takes 45 minutes to an hour.

Before I got on 41 at Fashion Valley Trolley Station Greenline.

I was talking to ICO from Naples,Italy on the S.D
Trolley at the Old Town Trolley Blue Line.

He said I spoke good Italian.

I see shrubbery and canyons then apartments or houses.

They are surrounded by hills.

I keep my mind active seeing the flowers and trees.

A guy on his motorcycle just passed by.

Life in the city of San Diego.

Another guy in a hot rod from the 1930s to 1940s.

Crisscrossing streets everywhere.

It's all in sequence.

I can see skyscrapers on the way.

One after the other steep up and down inclines of the way to VA.

Life through the eyes of the 41 Bus Route.

It interconnects everything.

I've passed here many times, young,old and not so old.

ALMOST TIME IMMEMORIAL LIKE THE RHYTHM OF LIFE IT SELF.

04/19/10

All Paths Lead To God.=Tous Le Chemins menent a Dieu

A word of Kind to be defined as content.=Un mot
de type être défini comme le contenu.

As I travel to my continent.=Comme je voyage sur mon continent.

Many paths lead toGod.=Beaucoup de chemins mènent à Dieu.

The end is one and the same.=La fin est un et le même.

For when is when I came.=Pour quand est quand comme je suis venu.

To be free as the wind free flowing spirit.=Pour être
libre comme le vent libère coule l'esprit.

To be at peace is what I merit.=Pour être à la paix est que je mérite.

Any creature of GOD deserves peace of mind.=N'importe
quelle créature de Dieu mérite la paix d'esprit.

we are to travel and unwind.=Nous sommes en
train de voyager et de nous dérouler.

All Paths Lead To GOD=Tous Le Chemins Mènent À DIEU.

How many days or nights must we endure to find release
from this world.=Combien de jours ou les nuits doivent
nous endurer à trouvons le relâchement de ce monde.

04/19/10

Oggi=Today

Today I will be okay and at peace.=oggi sarò giusto e alla pace.

My feelings will be content.=I miei sentimenti
saranno delle soddisfazioni.

Without resentment I will go on with my life.= Senza
il risentimento continuerò la mia vita.

I will look for the sweetness of things
.=Cercherò la dolcezza di cose.

To keep my mood and attitude happy.=Per tenere
il mio umore ed un'attitudine felice.

No more solitary confinement but out and
about with nature.=Nessun più isolamento ma
fuori da e di contatto con la natura.

Being one with humanity and nature is true peace=L'essere
uno con l'umanità e con la natura e la vera pace.

Like swimming a cocoon of water like an otter.- Come
nuotare un bozzolo di acqua come una lontra.

04/19/10

Muitas Coisas=Many Things

Many things to do, not enough time to do them.=Que
muitas coisas não fazem tempo suficiente para fazê-los.

I want to study my languages,singing,homework
and Judaism.=Quero estudar minhas
linguagens,cantar, dever de casa e Judaísmo.

But only so much that I can do in one day.=Mas
so tanto que posso fazer num dia.

I wish I had plenty of time to do it all.=Desejo ter abundância de tempo para fazê- lo todos.

Cooped up in study hall =Tran cafiou para cima em sala de estudo.

But time flies when you are keeping busy.=Mas tempo vai quando se mantém ocupado.

Is Life always on the run fast paced will it ever be replaced .=Esta vida sempre no jejum de corrida passe ou irão já é substituído.

04/19/10

A Las Eskondidas=In Hiding

Yo bivo komo djidio a las eskondidas=I live as a Jew in hiding.

Porke mi bida es mas kolay ansina=Because life is easier like this.

Dinguno save lo ke me afita si digo ke so djidyo.=No one
knows what happens to me if I say I'm Jewish.

Ay djente ke no bive ni desha bivir.=There are
people who don't live or let others live.

Eyos no respetan la fey,ni semsale ni el maale ande
biven los djidios.=The don't respect the faith ,nor
the race or square where the Jews live.

Por estas rasones kayadez ke sos djidio.=For these
reasons shut up about being Jewish.

Este es el legado Sefardi-Katoliko=This is the Sephardic-Catholic legend.

Agora ke abolti a la fey de Moshe.=Now I
returned to the faith of Moses.

Lu ke so yo es ser i bivir.=What I know s to be and live.

KryptoDjidio eskepto ande los muestros ser
djidio libremente.=CryptoJews accept where our
own are Jews in freedom of religion.

Ma en publiko so sekularo no avaro ma djidio libremente.=But
in public I am secular, not miserly but Jewish freely.

04/19/10

Musica=Music

La musica es mi vida.=Music is my life

Que me da la sangre para vivir.=That gives me blood to live.

Cuando canto y escucho me siento respirar.=When
I sing and hear I feel myself breathe.

Por el ritmo y vibra.=For the rhythm and vibration.

Me dan animo para saltar.= They give me life to jump.

Estoy feliz cuando oigo musica.= I am happy when I hear music.

Esta es la razón de mi vida .=This is the reason for my life.

Quiero cuando muera oir la musica.=When I
am dead I want to hear the music.

La música es mi flor que tiene mucho valor.=Music
is a flower that has much value.

Que muestra su esplendor.= That shows its splendor.

La música es mi dulce y delicia.= Music you are my candy and delicacy.

El manjar de los manjares todo o nada.=You are the
ambrose of all ambrosias, it's all or nothing.

Para mi la musica es todo.=For me music is everything.

04/19/10

Muchachika=Young Girl

Muchachika ande estaj yo vo a la plaj.=Damsel
where are you I go to the beach.

Me plazyo muncho ir a nadar en la mar.=It gave me
much pleasure to go swimming in the sea.

Al DIO kero rengrasyar.=To GOD I give thanks.

Muchachika ten pasensia komo estas asperar tu enrensia.=Miss
have patience like you are waiting for your inheritance.

Ven kerida a tomar el sol i sekarti de pyel.=Dear
come to sunbathe and dry your skin.

Serka la kosta de arena.= Go to the coast of sand.

Toma un poko d'agua ke agora tenesh sed.= Drink
a little water since now you have thirst.

Kome fruta ke tenesh ambre.=Eat fruit when you are hungry.

Muchachika deskansa ke estash karsa.=Damsel
rest because you are tired.

Muchachika tu eres bonika mas ke la morenika.=Young
woman you are more beautiful than the tanned one.

04/19/10

Rhythm

Rhythm is what I live for.

The fast heavy beat.

Increases my heart beat.

It fills my body with heat.

rhythm can I feel you in heavy metal.

Letting you go like the air.

I can hear it anywhere.

rhythm you are power in music.

You make me run fast.

So much I have a blast.

Let my blood curl oh rhythm you can twirl.

show me what you have got.

It's nothing similar to a spot.

The point of contention rhythm beats retention.

04/26/10

La Calle LLama=The Street Calls

Senti la musica Afro-Hispana=I felt the Afro-Hispanic Music.

Me dio por bailar el ritmo caliente.=I had a
hunch to dance the hot rhythm.

Yo y Maria bailamos en el Buena Vista Social Club.=Mary
and I danced at the Buena Vista Social Club.

Cancion De Cuba=Song Of Cuba.

En el festival camino de arte de Little Italy.= in
the festival walk of the Little Italy Art.

En San Diego.=In San Diego.

Quería cantar de nuevo relajado sin espanto=I wanted
to song a new relaxed without scarring.

Comimos en Filippis Pizzeria.= We ate at Filippis Pizzeria.

Senti el sol con calor yo estaba de humor.=I felt
the sun with warmth. I was in the mood.

Necesitaba la pluma y papel.=I needed the pen and paper.

Este evento magno avia de todo.=This magna event was everything.

Danza,canto,música,artesanías y arte fino incluso Bellas Artes.

La calle llama a mi alma y me llena de calma.=The
street called my soul and filled me with calm.

Yo quería bailar hasta que mis piernas se cansaran.=I
wanted to dance until my legs got tired.

El ambiente era una cosa sabrosa.=The ambience was a delicious thing.

Cada uno a su gusto hasta las señoras con su busto =Each
one to their own pleasure till the ladies with bust.

Bailamos en la calle sintiendo el ritmo como estar en
el abismo musical.=We danced in the street feeling
the rhythm like being in a musical abyss.

Oimos la musica de Quisqueya tremenda vaina se armo.=We heard the music of the Dominican Republic. A fierce problem was armed.

Sin cantar Huahuanco nosotros los latinos estamos en tarima.=Without singing Huahuanco we latins were on stage.

Felices de la vida cada quien con su pareja gozando.=Happy of life each one of the couples enjoyed.

Todos juntos vamos bailando.=Everyone together we were going to dance.

04/26/10

Vo Dar Lisiones=I Will Give Lessons

Vo dar lisiones.

Agora aspero al muevo chacham para ke me de
permisyon de dar lisiones de Ladino.=Now I wait for
the new Rabbi to let me give Ladino lessons.

Yo esto kontente ke Toivi yo vamos dar liston de Judezmo.=I was
content that Toivi and I were going to give lessons in Ladino.

Vo dar lisiones ke mientres reushita.= I am going
to give lessons while I await good use.

Las emosyones de mazal bueno me emosyono saver ke vo azer.=The
emotions of good luck had me emotional to know what to do.

Komo un melamed otra vez la djoya ke para mi es ambezar.=Like
a teacher another time the jewel for me to learn.

Lashon dulse vou dar lisiones a los djovenos i aedados.= I
will sweet talk to give lessons to the youth and elders.

Ke el DIO mos de berachot i chesed al buto ke tengo en tino.=May
GOD give us blessings and love to our objectives that I have in mind.

Es Ke vo de muevo outrun kamino.=Is that I go in a new road.

04/26/10

La Calle Llama=The Street Calls

Yo queria bailar hasta que mis piernas se cansaran=
I wanted to dance untill my legs got tired.

Senti la musica Afro-Hispana= I felt the Afro-Hispanic music.

El ambiente era una cosa sabrosa.= The ambience was a juicy thing.

Me dio por bailar el ritmo caliente.=It was a gut
feeling given to dance the hot rhythm.

Cada uno a su gusto.= Each one to thier pleasure.

Yo y Maria bailamos el Buena vista Social Club.= Mary
and I danced the Buena Vista Social Club.

Hasta las se~noras con su busto.= Even the ladies to thier bust.

Cancion De Cuba.= Song of Cuba.

Bailamos en la calle sintiendo el ritmo.= We
danced in the street feeling the rhythm.

En el Festival Camino De Arte de Little Italy como
estar en el abismo musical.=In the Festival of Art of
Little Italy like being in the musical abisymym.

En San Diego Oimos la musica de Quisqueya.=In San
Diego we heard the music of Hispaniola Island.

Queria cantar de nuevo relajado sin espanto tremenda
vaina se armo.=I wante to sing as of new relaxed
without fright tremendous ruckass was armed.

Comimos en Filippis Pizzeria sin cantar Huahuanco.= We
ate at Filippis Pizza Grotto without singing Huahuanco.

Senti el sol con calor yo estava de humor nosotros los
latinos estabamos en tarima.= I felt the sun with warmth
I was of humor we latins were on the stage.

Necesitava la pluma y papel felices de la vida.= I needed
the pen and paper we were happy of life.

Este evento magno avia de todo cada quien con su pareja gozando.= The magnanimous event was everything each one with thier other half enjoying.

Danza,canto,musica ,artesanias y arte firo incluso bellas artes.=Dance,song,music,arts and crafts ircluding Fine arts.

Todos juntos vamos bailando.= All of us together we go dancing.

La calle llama a mi alma me lleno de calma.=The street calls to my soul full of calm.

05/03/10

Le Coeur=The Heart

Le coeur est il un grande chose.=The heart is a great thing.

Je suis très heureuse quand mon coeur vive beaucoup.=I am very happy when my heart to live much.

Un chanson de mon anime et naissance un verre renaissance la vie en rose.=A song of my soul and birth a true rebirth the life in a rose.

Je crie que mon coeur est un rose.=I cry that my heart is a rose.

Que bataillez beaucoup de fois pour faire heureuz mais ils tres dure pour faitil toute les temps.=That battles much of times to make me happy it is hard to do that all the time.

Le coeur dans mon corps est très fort. =The heart is in my body very hard.

Je crois que c'est un défi à faire.=I think it is a challenge to do.

Toujours Prêt la joie de coeur.=Always the Joy of the heart.

La joie de vivre est beaucoup une part de mon coeur et ma vie.=The Joy of life is it much a part of my heart and my life..

Je voulez dit cet ca mon coeur.=I want to say thats it my heart.

05/03/10

Un Poema=A Poem

Un poema muevo es un desafío.=A new poem is a challenge.

Kadal diya manko palavrikas.=Each and every day I lack the little words.

Kel DIO me abedigua kon la faena ke tengo yo menester.=May
GOD bless me with the work that I have a need of.

Ke tengo komo fazer kapara kon gayina para pedron.=That I have
to do forgiveness offering with a chicken for forgiveness.

De los pekados ma es dulse komo el alkide kon almendras.=Of
the sins but it is sweet like the candy of almonds.

Yo kero reushita syempre ke me kita los poemas
agora.=I always want success with poems now.

Komo si huera dulsurya la poezia es anchura.=Like
it were candy , the poetry is thick.

Un manadero orijinalo di mi almika.= An
original source of my little soul.

De kita kolay a veses yuch.= It comes out easy at times difficult.

07/18/2011

Cosa Di Vita=Thing Of Life

La cosa di vita.= Thing of life.

La morte non mi piace!= Death does not please!

Quante volte la vita perduta!=How many times is life lost!

Gli cose alla morte.=The things to death.

Io vuoi cose buone per me.= I want good things for me.

Ed la mia famiglia.=And my family.

Molti ricordi belli.= Many beautiful memories.

Ma dove stai il mio vero amore la ragazza preferita?=but where is my true love the girl I prefer?

Facendo il seso sensuale per crescere una nuova vita come gli bambini.=Having sensual sex to give birth to a new life like the kids.

Una parola sol tanto basta.=Only saying the word is enough.

Andiamo al letto amore mio.= Let's go to bed my love.

Dammi un bacio e abbraccio.=Give me a kiss and hug.

Dolcemente ed forte.= Sweet and strong.

La vita finisce alle cento anni.=Life finishes in one hundred year

06/20/17

Desterrado=Exiled

Minha familha me destrói.=My family exiled me.

Meu sobrinho foi cabrao comigo.= My nephew was a cuckold with me.

Minha nae nao defenderme dou meu sobrinho.=My
mom did not defend me from my nephew.

Agora estou coitadinho eu detestou a minha
nae.=Now I am trouble I hate my mom.

Minha Familha sao filhos de puta comigo.= My
family are being S.O.B's with me.

Minha nae nao quer falar comigo =My mom
does not want to talk to me.

Minha pequenina irma unha puta comigo.=My
younger sister is a bitch to me.

Ela não castigou a meu sobrinho.=She did not punish my nephew.

Eu sou moito agravado com elas dois.i am
very angry with the two of them.

Xa não quero viver com minha nae Jamais.= Now I
don't want to live with my mom ever again.

Eu estou coitadinho minha familha sao cabroes comigo.=I
am trouble because my family are cuckolds with me.

Estou isolado do minha sangue.=I am isolated
by those of my own blood relatives.

01/04/18

Music

Music takes my boredom away its ah takes my breath away.

It keeps me happy so it makes me snappy.

Music is the balm for my soul .

Hearing it hunts a troll.

It makes me dance and snap my fingers.

Even though I'm not a singer.

I forget my troubles keep me positive no more negative.

However one is light hearted as they enjoy the music.

We keep ourselves content, no lament.

01/08/23

Montare

Montare is an eclair .

8 Months long of my life.

I learned so much which is such.

About fixed and growth mind set.

Do you wanna bet.

Maturity in great stride the staff is filled with pride.

From February 3rd to Cinco De Mayo.

I did not go to Ohio.

Back August 28th to the present the lights are on its luminescent.

So many coping skills I thought they were drills.

Experience is what I will instill in myself.

I'm 5ft7in not an elf.

To many topics the weather is not in the tropics.

In the future I look forward to sending real dreams upward.

9/4/23

Muncho Pedri= Much I Lost

Muncho pedri sin mi madri=I have lost much without my mother.

Agora esto en shok non so Belle Epoque.= Now
I am in schock I am not Belle Epoque.

La djente ande moro dizin al Dyo yoro.= The
people where I live say to GOD I cry.

Dinguno savi ke asperar di mi =No one knows what to expect of me.

Ken disho esto ansi?= Who said it like this?

Agora pyedro la ora! = Now I lose the hour!

Dimi porke sinyora!=Tell me why mam!

Todo o nada a kapa o espada.= It's all or nothing with a cape or sword.

Ya non so manseviko ni chikitiko.= I am not a young man or a babe.

Kave o tchay de bevyenda.= Coffee or tea as the drink.

Esto ke komi merienda.= It's like I eat a snack.

No sto en la kaza ke me pasi.=I am not at home that I passed by.

En letcho stranyo non durmi.= In bed I did not sleep.

Ande sta mi mazal? =Where is my luck?

Onde mora mi madre en arabal.=Where does my mom live in a suburb.

9/4/23

Hope

I hope for better things in the future.

My poetry is a source of my culture.

Inspiration is my radiation.

When I dreamo it's my chemo.

Hope not dope is the kaleidoscope.

With hope I can Cope.

Hope is huge, bigger than an antelope.

I dream in streams through the beams of hope.

I'm alive not a stroke.

From White to Black folk.

Hope is a fire I will stoke.

To be inspired hope has hired it is something to be acquired.

It seems happy to hope I'm at the beginning of the rope.

Hope means not to mope its yes not nope.

9/5/23

La Monta~na Verde =The Green Mountain.

Me puedo ver en verde de hierbas.=I can see myself in green of herbs.

Comulgar con la naturaleza.= To commune with nature.

Todo el foliaje esta espezo.=All the foliage is thick.

De un sendero a otro veo Esmeralda's.= From
one trail to another I see emeralds.

Desde ligero a muchas cargas. = From light to heavy loads.

Aire fresco el brote del monte de un azote. =Fresh
air sprouts of the mountain whipping.

Ramas y verdulagas entrenzados en la matiz.=Branches
and purslane intertwined in the hue.

En el verdor se puede ver la raiz.=In the green you can see the root.

No hay casi nada para comer pero esta mucho en engrandecer.=There
is hardley anything to eat but there is much to grow.

Hay Flora y fauna que no se muestra mucho por esto yo escucho.=
There Flowers and wildlife it doesn't show much for this I hear.

La imensidad de la monta~na que le falta mucho la ca~na.=
The immensity of the mountain that lacks much cane.

A pensar que todo esto era de Espa~na.=To
think all this belonged to Spain.

Un poquito yo mancito lo verde del campo yo repito.= A
little bit I am tender the green of the camp I repeat.

9/5/23

Os Tempos=The Times

Os tempos que lembran sao un pe¯doa.= The
times that remember are a forg veness.

Na cancao nao e boa. = The song is rot beautiful.

Muito asperamos que temos dancando.= We are
waiting much that they are dancing.

A gente vai andando.= The people are walking.

Sempre acho um poquinho.=I always think a little.

Chauzinho a voce em o caminho.= Bye to you on the road.

Ninguem sabe pra quei qui eu lembrei.=
Noone knows for what I remember.

Forca do povo e que somos.= Force of the people and that we are.

Os dias passam pra mim nao voltam.= The
days pass for me don't return.

Por isso vamos a paraiso.=For that we go to paradise.

Lembrou porque estou sozinho por mais eu vou lembrais?.=
Remember why I was alone for more I went do you remember?

Sentindo que acho abaixo!.=I feel that I am thinking below!

Agora voultei e que andei.= Now I return, and I walked.

Ninhum fala como uma bala.= Noone talks like a bullet.

Como bacalhau do Macau. = Just like cod of Macau.

9/5/23

Io Lo So= I know This

Io lo so che non mangio.= I know that I eat this.

Che succedeno avanti.= What occurs before.

Come Dante- Like Dante.

Nessuno sapeva =No One knows.

Una sorte di bella= A kind of beauty.

Non ce capeva.=That is not understood.

La signorina e carina== The miss is a dear.

Mangiamo noi in cucina.=We eat in the kitchen.

Tutto questo e per la mattina.= All this for the morning.

Sempre di mente di la gente.= Always the mind of the people.

Capiremo allo il estremo.=Understand to the extreme.

Ciao a tutti non volemo.= Goodbye to everyone we don't want.

Io lo so non ho capito.= I don't have understand.

Il mio esprito.=It is my spirit.

Allora vene se vede molti.=Now you come it is seen a lot.

Sono Io chi ascolti.= It is I who listens.

9/10/23

Le Ferrier=The Furcoat Man

Le ferrier que admire jackette de technologie.=The fur
coat man that admires the jackette of technology.

Beaucoup de danger pour moi je ne sais pas.=
Much danger for me I don't know.

Non ou la la!=No wow!

Je suis moqueur avec mon figuré c'est très dure.=
I am laughter with my face very hard.

Pour moi la technologie est l'ordonnateur de l'
internet mais il très mauvais.=For me the technology
is the computer of internet the very bad

Pasque j'ai doleur me gratter le coeur ...'avais en petite
doleur.=Because I have pain it cuts the heart. I have a little pain.

Laissez Moi silvouplait pourquois je
pleurait.=Leave me please because I cry.

9/10/23

The Crown

Peaceful calm song in an opera house.

Inspiration of an epic during WWII of Later immigrants who
come to America beating the odds in a new country.

9/10/23

Mars

Erie sound of mystery. Like the discovery of Atlantis. This fills me with hope.A harpsichord yet ominous profound sound. Sirens calling all the sailors to dive off ship to land in the sunken continent. Full of treasures and sea animals as well as a new king.

9/10/23

The Kiss

Celtic music Emerald Isle Irish kilts like Scotland. Bagpipes,violins,flutes,drums,guitars, harps. Caildeah for the green fields of Galicia,Asturias and Brittany.A chant to the ancestors.

Celebrations of Halloween and St.Patricks With a music festivals In Lorient,Bridttany ,France including Cantabria and Celtic nations.It's the story of my Paternal greatgreatgrandfather Leandro Coronel Irish and Spanish Jew.

9/10/23

Futebol=Soccer

Ronaldinho joga pelo Real Madrid muito importante.=Ronaldo
that plays for the Royal Madrid is very important.

Melhor atleta da Espanha.= The best athlete of Spain.

Um grau de experiência para trabalhar por uma pensão.=
A degree of experience for working for a pension.

Tudo isso pra mim diz muito que neste mulatinho e excelente jogador.=
All that for me says much that this biracial is an excellent player.

Como é mencionado mais que eu acho ele um bom atleta da Europa.=
Like is mentioned more than that I think he is good athlete of Europa.

Todo mundo disputa por ele.= All of the world disputes for him.

Ronaldo entrou no que lembrou que estou achando sozinho.=
Ronaldo trained to that memory of him was thinking alone.

Tchauzinho os televidentes que tem em mente.=Goodbye
to the tv viewers that have him in mind.

De repente ele volta ao Brasil pra seleção Nacional pra
jogar os olímpicos.= Suddenly he returns to Brazil for
the National Selection to play in the Olympics.

Ronaldo e campeao do Real Madrid.= Ronald
is champion of Real Madr d.

Neste homem que tingiu pra fazer um ganhador com estudo
e força do treinamento ganhou sua posição na Europa do
Oeste.=This man that has to make a winner with study and
force of training winning his position of Western Europe.

Brasil quantos Ronaldos tem para prevalecer a seus competidores.=
Brazil how many Ronalds do you have to beat your competitors.

9/18/23

Posicio=Position

Jo sóc una mistura de gents.= I am a mixture of peoples.

Cada vegada vull anar amb la família.=Each
time I want to be with my family.

Obrir meu cor tingui molts amor por meva poble i ciutat.= I open
my heart because it has lots of love for my people and city.

Ninguém sabia que violem o jornal de diumenge non si.=
Noone knew that violated the journal of Sunday yes no.

No disatbe per ir al kal Juic ou Montjuic.= Not Saturday to
go to the Jewish synagogue or Mountain of the Jew.

Un Rabbi parla a les Xuetes de Balears Mallorca i
Menorca.=A rabbi spoke of the Crypto Jews or Chuetas
of Balearic Islands Majorca and Minorca.

Dintre meu cor parlo una mica de Tora i Talmud.= Inside
my heart spoke a little of Torah and Talmud.

Ara podeu veure les mullers cantant el shalom alechem sense la
biblia Catolica perque les Xuetes soc Judeus de veritat.= Now you
can see the women sing peace be upon you without a Catholic
bible because the CryptoJews the Chuetas are truly Jewish.

Ningu sapiga mes que molts de Judeus.=Noone
knows more than all the Jews.

Parlarem,convertire e faram alia a Israel.= We shall speak
of,convert to Judaism and send them to Israel.

Nuria es Nurit, Maria es Miriam,Miquel es Michael,Josep
es Joseph totalment canvi el origen.= Nora is Nurit,Mary is
Miriam,Mike is Michael,Joe is Joseph totally changes origin.

Que lo Judeo Parla Fort L'església està tancat i la
Keila se obrin.=The Judaism speaks very loud the
church is closed and the Temple is open.

La Porta es gran per les que vull tornar al Judaisme les ancestres.=The door is big for those who want to return to Judaism of the ancestors.

Jo soc qui soc sol Deu sap meva estoria.= I am who only God knows my story.

9/18/23

Pienso=I Think

Yo pienso mucho en lo que haré si yo no cantare.=I
think much about what I would do if I didn't sing.

Alabando a Dios el dia honrado.= To God praise the day is honored.

Porque pensar en el ayer es lo que quieres saber.= Why
do you think yesterday is what you wanted to know?

Yo recojo todo con mis ojos sin tener antiojos.= I pick
up everything with my eyes without contacts.

Tengo lo que se va traspasar porque pensaré
cómo voy a solucionarlo.=I have what will be
trespassed why I shall think how to solve it.

El día para mi se mide según lo que sentía no pienso Maria.=The
day is measured according to what I felt not thinking about Mary.

Muchos son que me han cerrado los confines sin andar en patines.=
Many are the ones who have closed the ends without being on skates.

Yo doy vueltas a que se me abren las puertas.=I
make turns to that my doors are open.

Porque pienso mucho es a ti te escucho.= Because
I think much of it is you to whom I listen.

Pienso es un avenir que puedo decir.= I think
it is a reconcile what can I say.

Todo se volteo para mi bien pensar.= Everything
changed for better thinking.

Es a mi que le van a dar.=It is to me that they are going to give.

Pienso yo no soy menso.= I think I'm not stupid.

9/25/23

5years/House Rules/House

After 5 years I picture myself very happy. Living in my house with my wife and children is not snappy. I will have friends as well as family in our home.I will be free to roam. I will only have one sexual partner, my wife. It will be a very nice life. Children to pass down traditions in merry conditions. My education will improve me to a business position.Speaking,working in foreign languages. Having lunch tri tip sandwiches.A home cooked meal from my woman for me. All worries cast aside in voyages or trips national or international giving tips. Me, my woman moving our hips. My family will grow children,grandchildren so forth naming from my lips.

10/10/23

Musica Galega=Galician Music

Coa as gaitas eu escoito do moito.= With the bagpipes I hear a lot.

Ninguen me diches porque eu cantu.=Noone tells me why I sing.

Mi~nas lembranzas de rapaci~no.= My memories of my youth.

Todolos neno vai atopar una nena.= Every boy is going to find a girl.

Para min nacin o corazon unho amori~no.=For
me a love is born in my heart.

As cousas estanche craras e nobreza.=The things are clear and noble.

Moitas grazas muller eu amoche.= Many thanks woman I love you.

Graci~nas Deus por meu vida.= Thanks God for my life.

Cartos se vindo a min benvindo.=Money is seen to me welcome.

As bendicions d'alma cal e tua?= The blessings
of the soul what is yours?

Todas meus razons e o cerebro e corazon.= All
my reasons and the brain and heart.

Dous mares te~nans peixes para pesca.=The
two seas have fish for the catch.

A Deu eu ten que agradezca.= Oh God I have you to thank.

Ninhun vou con min o meu camin.=Noone goes with me or my road.

Sentindo os raios de meus ensaios.= Feeling the rays of my rehearsal.

Na saeta vai a ti compreta.= The arrow goes to you complete.

10/10/23

Hoy No Quise Ir Con Los Caballos=Today I Did
Not Want to Go with The Horses.

Hoy no quise ir con los caballos. = I did not want to go with the horses.

Porque las moscas me molestan y los caballos las
detestan.=Because the flies bug me, and the horses hate them.

Aun tres caballos tienen terapia en comun.= Even
though three horses have therapy in common.

Primera Vez me alborote mas ni hice disparate. = First
time I had rampage, but I did not do nonsense.

Ninguno le gustan las moscas que alguno not le importa!=
Noone likes the flies that one does not care!

Para mi la situacion es que no se soporta.= For me
the situation is that I cannot withstand it.

Siempre estamos con la naturaleza.= We are always with nature.

Rodeaos de arboles,matas, y flores. = Surrounded
by trees, shrubs, and flowers.

De colores de todas hojas verdes.= All the colors of the green leaves.

Cuando voy yo tengo que tener cuidado.=
When I go, I have to be careful.

El corral es en el mismo condado.= The yard is in the same county.

Hay un caballo negro y blanco ademas de una potra casta~na.=
There are a black and white horses also a chestnut mare.

Son buenos pero tienen sus ma~nas.=They
are good, but they have their tricks.

Ya que son lindos animales mas con errores pueden ser fatales.
=They are beautiful animals but with errors can be deadly.

10/10/23

I'm tired I want to rest from manure I attest.

The flies are bothersome with this house threesome.

Today I did not want to go to the corral for it has affected my morale!

These horses are Beautiful, but the b lack
one like taking apples from a tree.

I didn't like that I didn't have an apple for the chestnut female horse.

I felt a lot of remorse.

I decided to take a break from the farm
even though there was no harm.

These animals are therapeutic.

I see they keep it copasetic.

There was a dog and two women no men.

I was impressed how simple there horses were triple.

10/20/23

I Want Connection

I want connection not retrospection.

The year I was born is my conception.

That between woman and man, woman to
woman, man to man relation.

Traditional and untraditional adult couples to mention.

Right now, my love life is in suspension.

Too many toxic relationships have caused erosion.

I need to love myself before others into love motion.

For it's as if I don't know the story of which I have no notion.

It is for me like I'm drowning in the ocean.

Lets fight for my life not abortion.

To me it is a metal screw in corrosion.

So you see I want connection.

10/21/23

Arrelumbra El Sol= The Sun Is Lit Up

Veo Plantas que arrelumbra.= I see plants that light up.

No tan blanco como el marmol.= It is not white like marble.

Una cordillera de montes que no quiero montar de esto te digo al contar.=A mountain chain that I don't want to ride. I tell you to count.

Animales como tarántulas;ara~nas,ardillas,víboras,y leon montes sin zapatillas.=Animals like tarantulas,spiders,squirrels,snakes and mountain lions without slippers.

Hay muchos árboles que apodar los troncos a se los vas a dar.= there are many trees that need pruning. Who are you giving the trunks?

La naturaleza cura las pesadillas andar con los animales entre comillas.=Nature cures the nightmares to go with animals between brackets.

Preciso el brillo de los rayos solares De pies ante Dios en los altares.=I need the shine of the solar rays on the feet before God on the altars.

Si Hubiera miel silvestre de sus manjares si lo comes te repares.= If there were wild honey ambrosia if you ate like it fixed.

Hermoso las flores perfumadas es así que vienen las hadas.= Beautiful the perfumed flowers it 's like this that the fairies come.

El subir y bajar la cordillera de Santa Mónica se oye los chapulines su sinfoncia.= The going up and going down of the Santa Monica mountain chain you can hear the the crickets symphony.

Las aves vuelan contentas buscando sabor a menta.=The birds fly happily searching for the flavor of mint.

10/28/23

Dear PoP

I miss you much. I'm always thinking of you. When people smoke or I meet other combat vets, not all Vietnam Vets. I wish I could have told you I was bisexual but you would have disowned me. I am overcoming my obstacles one day at a time. Pop When I see fish I picture you at the pier with your pole and chum hearing los Churumbeles. I remember when you had flashbacks how you drank to drown them and we had to touch the temple of your head. You loved us but you were strict with me. I will never forget you or your legacy of Nam and family history wherever you are in heaven. I'm thinking you suffer no more.

11/06/23

Verita/Truth/Verdad/Verdade

La verita costa quando si dice.=Truth costs when you say it.

No lo so di che per me è difficile.= I don't know of is difficult for me.

Nessuno conosce la situazione.=Noone knows why.

Allora ma Ancora ando Io.= Now and still I go.

When one says the truth they can be killed of which i'm not thrilled.

They say the truth will set you free but then you have to hide you see.

La realidad decir la verdad es bruta la verdad es una fruta fatal.=The reality to say the truth is brutal, the truth is a fatale fruit.

Nadie puede vivir sin peligro por eso yo me resigno y emigró.= Noone can live without danger for that I resign and emigrate.

A verdade pra min nao e saudade porque isto dura uma eternidade.=The truth for me is it does not and is nostalgia because it is hard to last eternity.

Muito eu perdido com o peito A verdade se tinha muito respeito.= I have lost a lot with the chest the truth it has a lot of respect.

11/06/23

Trust

How do I trust people? When I've been thrust with evil deception
to mention.I ask myself will I ever trust again. The bank gave me
a bad spin.I'm in a precarious situation waiting sigh intonation. I
have this for introspection .So your view I can't trust is true. Evil
people who do you screw? I have lost my trust in others. Why
bother? I am going to be very selective and very perceptive. I know
someday I will go. Trust GOD to know I will grow. In the Holy Books
I will look. One day GOD will improve my lot even if people plot.
I have many holy alternatives to trust believers not deceivers.

11/17/23

Dia Dorado=Golden Day

Ya tengo mi día dorado de Mónaco al principado.= I have
my golden day from Monaco to the principality.

Es con oro comparado .= It is like gold compared.

A mi me gusta el champurrado.= I like champurrado.

La vía al estrado.= the way to the platform.

Que viene el señor Alvarado.= That Mr.Alvarado is coming.

A veces pienso en mi ahijado.= At times I think of my god-son.

Solo el Dio me busca un hado.= Only God finds me a fate.

Solo el dia soleado.= Only the sunnified day.

De rosas esta floreado.= Of roses it is blooming.

11/17/23

Le Jour Au Soleil=Sunny day

Le jour au soleil est une merveille.=The day of sun is a marvel.

Laquele c'est la belle.= It is the beauty.

Une etoile n'est pas mal.= The star is not bad.

Chacune manger une prune.= Of which I eat a dried plum.

La vie continuee' pour le jeune passe!=Life
continues for the young to pass.

Une jour questque cest avec l'ete.=A day that is with summer.

J'alle bien pour commencee non est une menage etrangere.=
I go well to begin it is not a strange cleaning.

11/17/23

Rage

I do not know the causes of why I rage .It's not pleasant nor a stage. I have victims pent up anger and frustration the sources of which are an amalgamation.Hate crime I' m lost in time. Rape , Murder,Blanket Party does not Rhyme. Buried hatred in the shed so depressed I lie in bed. When will I heal as my soul squeals.

11/20/23

The New Ysmael

The new ysmael controls his anger with prudence,forgiveness,
go getter. Is sure of himself in school,with women romantically.
By being forgiving and using logic his rage disintegrates
to syncopate. The new Ysmael is not codependent. I am
whole and completely loving myself shower,brushteeth.
ADL's shaves,trims nails and a pedicure uses cologne and
deodorant. He looks to GOD forward to his future in his life.

11/20/23

5 Love Languages

Physical touch-sex,cuddling,hand on the thigh or shoulder.

Active service-Helping out ,unconditionally.

Token of Affections-Gifts

Quality Time- Non-sexual intimacy

Words of Affirmation-Terms of endearment.

11/20/23

Love Language/Lengua De Amor

Que es bonit acariciar a tu pareja

Yes to cuddle on the couch kissing.

She or he helps me clean or organize the
house,sin que esperen algo a cambio.

Le doy regalos de valor sentimental,I appreciate
their smiles on their birthday.

Estando juntos íntimamente jugando cartas,without sex.

I love you honey,palabras que confirman nuestro amor.

11/22/23

Friendships

What type do you want ?Loyal,
Compassionate,compromises,patient,considerate,unselfish.

What kind of values do they have?Spiritual,kindness,brings and takes
from the table,productive, positive,uplifting,meditate every morning.

12/03/23

Where do I want to go? How I'm going to achieve it.A Poem

I want to rise to the top 123 and I hop.

Me with courage and determination is motivation you cannot stop.

Get an education from a nation and do it on my laptop.

I want business acumen for when I go to temple
I say amen of the spiritual crop.

I take an internship for my labor to fix work up the ladder and not lop.

Smell the aroma of a high school diploma as you say what's up.

I feel I'm achieving because I'm dreaming I can't be bought.

Finishing my education so I can not be distraught is my relation.

I am wise to futurise I know I'm taught.

Me with my associates,bachelors and masters not the barrister I'm hot to trot so say fortune is coming is it running I will have my way.

01/08/24

16 things To Do When I'm Getting Mad NotTo Blow Up

1)Go to McDonalds Mom diet coke.Tia Trine
Ice cream cone and me a coke.

2)Go for a scenic drive on highway 101 in Northern San
Diego County along the coast from Oceanside.

3)Go To The store.

4)Go to the park.

5)See a friend.

6)Listen to music.

7)Write a poem.

8)Count to ten.

9)Meditate.

10)Breathing exercises.

11)Go to my room on my comouter.

12)Go to the Old Town Temecula Museum.

13)Call a friend.

14)Call the warmline.

15)PRR

16)ACE

01/12/24

Frio=Cold

Este frío es inaguantable que a mi no me da ganas de baile.= This cold is unbearable and does not give me the will to dance.

Estoy frígido en las aguas heladas sumergido.=I am frigid submerged in cold waters.

Yo estoy tomando leche,café, té o chocolate sin pegar una bola con bate.=I am drinking milk, coffee, tea or chocolate without hitting a ball with a bat.

Quien quiere comer batido con el intenso helor fallecido que me olvido.= Who wants to eat a shake like an intense cold died out that I forget.

6 meses todos con catarros al punto que tenemos barro.=6 months with a cold to the point we have mud.

Champurrado dulce achocolatado se ha disfrutado.=Champurrado sweet with chocolate is enjoyed.

No mas sudor en las sueras y pantalones que necesitamos blancos polvorones para los pies no calzones.=No more sweat in the sweaters and pants that we need white polka dots for the feets not underwear.

Resfrio en trio ya perdió el brillo.= Cold in a trio I have lost the shine.

Ahora nos bañamos con el sol acurrucados calientes en caracol.= Now we bathe with the sun snuggled warm in the snail.

No es primavera para comer girasol es quimera de mármol.=It is not spring for me to eat sunflower it is chimera of marble

Nadie quiere el frío ni a mi o el tío.=Noone likes the cold, not me or the guy.

01/15/24

Aspero Ir Al Kal = I Wait To Go To The Synagogue

Asperar para orasyonar kon el haham.= To wait to pray with the rabbi.

Vijitaremos el kal las mujeres guizando kon su delantal.= We will visit the synagogue of the women cooking with thier apron.

Todo vyernes de chabat empesijamos la kumida ke no kedesh en su mida.= Every Friday of Shabbat we start the food that does not stay in its measure.

Kezo i peshe se asemeje algu kon kashkaval i levadura al pan kon sal.= Cheese and fish that resembles hard cheese and bread without leaven and salt.

La Mellah inchida de famiyas i amistades es komo aharvar los portalles.= La Jewish quater is filled with families and friends is like knocking the gates.

Dinguno savi la recheta di mi madri sol tanto ke goza mi padri.= Noone knows the recipe that of my mother only that my father enjoys.

O Adonai ke nos liberasti del Sinai ansi mozos tuvimos nasyon porke estuvimos en tu korason.= O GOD that you freed us of the Sinai we had a nation because we were in your heart.

Muncho fraguamos lo fruchiguozos kantes en el altar.=Much we built the flourishing songs in the altar.

Al Dio grasiya loar= To GOD thanks to give thanks.

Syempre me asentari a Yerushalayim al muro de yanto kotel Maariv tefila i tsedaka kon la djente ke non tyeni parnasa para komer solo los andjelos su amaneser.=I will always sit towards the wall of wailing the western wall prayer and charity the people that don't have to eat only the angels there sunrise.

01/15/24

Sephardic Jew 1492

I descend from 1492 Spain 1497 Portugal.I've been denied recognition
by the Israeli government citizenship,Immigration to Eretz. I go to
synagogue to commune with my ancestors that suffered persecution
by the Catholic church. I am a jew through and true. Ask me why
I am not in Israel bye. I have been abandoned,marginalized and
forsakenThe Ashkenazim are obliterating our history,culture,Sephardic
Judaism including Ladino, taking our women and discriminating
against Sephardim. Anusim don't have nothing from Sephardim.We
want Sephardic Judaism,Ladino and culture.The Ashkenazim Are the
new vulture.If antisemitism did not exist we would have a civil war
in Eretz between Ashkenazim against other Jews and Sephardim.I
feel the rejection internally as well as externally.I am disillusioned
in Israel that for us anusim its a deathbell to hell. We are strangers
to other Jews and our own Sepharadim.I am not truly accepted by
the Orthodox Sephardim. I'm bereft by our people that deny me
a Sephardic Orthodox conversion. I study and understand Ladino
since I am Latino. My heart is sad because my world is being forced
to assimilate into Ashkenazi. Ashkenazim have everything on a silver
platter to them and Orthodox Sephardic, the Anusim don't matter
since we are not white they underestimate us in being bright

01/19/24

Next Goals For Leaving Montare

1)I need to explore the reasons behind my anger.

2)Tolerance of the Samuel's of the world.

3)Publish my 2nd book of poetry.

4)Start a payment plan to pay back Financial
Aid and VA Ch 31at $50 a month.

5)Go back to adult school for an entire semester.

6)No more Summer semesters in college and the
university Spring and Fall semesters only.

7)Get back to DBSA Temecula,CR,synagogue,Christian
friends,friends and family,VA,AA and Coda inlcluding
Montare online as well as core.College &Adult School.

8)Get along with family & friends.

9)I will not drink spiritsand soda unless I have to.

10)Deal with the fiduciary Payee battle.

11)Accept the payee if I lose and make it positive.

12)Learn to budget my money better for my own good.

13)Showering everyday,shaving, doing laundry,
washing my underwear separately.

14)Keeping my room clean and organized.

15)Taking my meds,vitamins and natural supplements on time.

16)Wake up early at 7 or 8 am and sleep after taking meds at 8 or 9 pm.

17)Going to synagogue on shabbat,visiting the
church with my Christian friends to tolerate other
religions,countries,ethnic groups, the Golden Rule

18)Study new books of Sephardic Judaism,Sephardic
History,Improve Judeo Spanish.

19)Improve my 6 languages and learn
Hebrew,Arabic and other languages.

20)Set personal boundaries in all my relationships,family
friends,fellow students as well as coreligionists and
Authority figures so I avoid misunderstandings.

21)Do a checklist of my daily goals or written poetry
deadline to my publishers production team.

22)As I am Inspired by life, I produce poetry, paints,ceramics
etc to do with Art and vacation to prevent burn out.

01/19/24

El Cambio Por Poesia= The Change for Poetry

Quiero cambiar el mundo versus mis poemas.=I
want to change the world versus my poems.

Mi vida una antología es el lema.=My life is an anthology. It is a challenge.

Mi poesía puede generar arte visual,Video,Bellas Artes Finas y artes
de baile,canto,piezas de teatro y música además canciones.=My
poet can generate visual art,video,Fine Arts and the Performing arts
like singing,dancing , theatre pieces and music including songs.

Por esto creo cambiar el mundo por estas razones.= For
this I think it can change the world for these reasons.

Contribuir a la cultura del mundo es mi escultura.=Contribute
to the culture of the world. It is my sculpture.

Para la sociedad de acuerdo a los temas es lo que inspira mis
poemas.= For society according to the themes it inspires my poems.

Cuando sue~no es en grande en un instante.='When I dream it is big.

Es lo que tengo en mi mente mi poesia contribuir a la
cultura del lejano Oriente.=What I have in mind for my
poetry to contribute to the culture of the far east.

Aunque no viva mas mi poesia dejo atras.= Even though I
don't live on but it will be my poetry I leave behind.

Sere rico y famoso como una leyenda un cafe y pan
dulce es mi merienda. = I will be rich and famous like
a legend a coffee and sweet bread is my picnic.

Bollywood,Hollywood y Broadway serán mis productoras
de mis poemas en peliculas o piezas de teatro.=
Bollywood,Hollywood and Broadway will be my producers
of my poems into movies or theatre scripts.

Es con mis poemas serenata al mundo entero por esto le
pido a DIOS esto yo tolero.= It is with my poem serenade to
the entire world for this is what I ask GOD I tolerate.

2/24/2024

Corazon Solitario.= Solitary Heart

Hay un poquito de amor= There Is A Little Of Love

Tengo amor dentro mi corazón.= I have love in my heart.

Un amor desconocido muy lejos de mi.= A
love unknown very far from me.

Solo se que no la encuentro aqui cerquitas aqui.=
I only know that I don't live near here.

No se como se llama ni el nombre de su raza.= I don't
know what it is called or the name of her race.

Podrá tener caridad.= Will have charity.

No se ni a su raza.= I don't even know or even her race.

O ella acaso de mi edad.= Or is she even of my age.

En donde vive cuál es su país.= Where she
lives and what is her country.

Yo la presiento como mi raíz feliz.= I feel like a happy root.

Yo no miento por no ser feliz.= I don't lie because I'm not happy.

Corazon Solitario= Solitary Heart

Tengo amor dentro mi corazon.= I have love in my heart.

Hay un amor desconocido muy lejos de mi.= I
have an unknown love very far from me.

Solo se que no la encuentro cerquita de aqui.=
Only I know I don't find her near here.

Podra tener caridad o es ella de mi edad en donde podrá.=Will
she have charity or is she of my age in which she will.

No se como se llama ni el nombre de su raza.= I don't
know what she is called or the name of her race.

Podra tener caridad o es ella de mi edad.= Could
she have charity or is she my age.

318

En donde vive y cuál es su país.= Where does
she live and which is her country.

No la mire pero me hace feliz.= I don't see but she makes me happy.

Es algo que presiento y no miento.= It is something I feel and I don't lie.

No te desesperes corazon solitario.= Don't despair solitary heart.

Ya hallarás como bendito relicario.= You will find like a blessed riliquary.

2/24/2024

Chuva=Rain

Chuva,chuva à noite durante uma seca=Rain,rain in the night of a dry.

Cinco anos inteiros de seca.= 5 entire years of drought.

Tão bem na guerra se acabar na luta durou sete meses.=It
is good the is finishing the struggle lasted 7 months.

Por fim, um pouco de paz.= At last a bit of peace.

Eu sinto que neste ano seria bom que neste ano.= I
feel that this year shall be better than this year.

Meu primo voa minha pra viver com mim.=
MY cousin will fly to live with me.

Não sei se tenho irmão.= I don't know if I have a brother.

2/24/2024

Dirme Perché=Tell me

Dirme perché te piace.= Tell me why it pleases you?

Quando lo te bace.= When I kiss you.

Ed di questo tu saprai.= And the what you shall know.

Che a lei te amerai.=That I will love you.

Io so,Io so Io so Io so.=I know,I know,I know,I know.

Una donna come e la chimera per me.= A
woman that is like a chimera for me.

Suspire da verte.= I sigh when I see you.

2/24/2024

Desenvolver= Uninvolved

Saia da tristeza da minhalma.= Out goes the sadness of my soul.

Ainda não sei porque não fazer amizade e enamorada.=
Even not I am why not make friendship and love.

Sempre sozinho pra viver.= Always alone for what to live.

Sempre no arapos de o ver em tudo me sinto triste.=
Always the foxes of the seeing in every me feeling sad.

Em tudo meu sinto triste que querc chorar.= In
everything I feel sad that I want to cry.

Da desesperação está em mim.= Of the desperation is in me.

Eu morro de amor, eu morro por aceitação.=
I die of love,I die por acceptance.

Estão sempre em minha cabeça. = I am always in my head.

Penso em isso tudo tempo ainda que estar no exílio.=
I think all the time even though I'm in exile.

Não tem que lutar com minha gerte.= I don't
have to fight with my people.

2/24/2024

Ensename= Show Me

Ensename a amar.= Show me how to love.

Ensename a convivir.= Show me how to break bread.

Como acabar esta timidez.= How to finish this timidness.

Desnudez social irreal emocional.= Nakedness social unreal emotional.

Yo te necesito.= I need you.

Tu que no estas aqui.=You that are not here.

Dentro de mí hay un vazio.=Inside of me there is a void.

Que le falta su brio.= That lacks the shine.

Un hombre no es completo hasta que tenga su mujer.= A man is not complete without till he has his woman.

Solo,Soltero.= Alone, Bachelor.

No se sabe su paradero.= No he does not know his destiny.

2/24/2024

Je Desirez= I Desire

Je desirez le femme que etil de bon etrangere. =
I desire a woman who is a good foreign.

Vous non ettes de mon pay.= You are not from my country.

Le monde est comme un ombre.= The world is like a shadow.

Un bete noire nouve de femme et beau.= A
black beast new of woman and beauty.

Je ne sais pas pourquoi.= I don't know why.

Je verrai un jour.= I see a day.

Le femme marche pour la tour Eiffel.=The
woman marches for the Eiffel tower.

Oui,Oui ,Oui OU est mon paramour.= Yes,yes,yes where is my love.

J'ai la demoiselle le quinze jour.=I have Miss the 2 weeks.

Il s' appelle Marisol.= Who is called Marisol.

Elle ou un femme Portugaise.= She is a Portuguese woman.

Les yeux coloriel et blue.= The eyes are colored and blue.

Je marche pour les Champs Elysee.=I walk for the Elysian Fields.

Je marche con moi femme le semaine denier faite accompli.=
I walk with my wife the week last accomplished fact.

Lembrança Da Pesca= Memory of Fishing

Meu pai gosta de pesca todas as manhãs as tardes,as noites=My father likes fishing all the mornings the afternoons and nights.

Salinhas peixões um dia ele consegue oito peixes.= Salty fish one day he gets 8 fishes.

Pra mim é bom e uma boa ideia.= For me it is a good idea.

Eu recordo quando era menino tão bem pescava e caminhava para comprar na carnada.=I remember when I was young too I well fished and walked to buy bait.

Lembrando encantador bom homem vendo a mim um peixe por quinze centavos.= I remember an enchanting good man who sold me a fish for 15 cents.

Quando era um pouco mais eu queria dar algo a um pelicano pra alimentação.= When I was a little more I wanted to give something to give to a pelican some nutrition.

2/27/24

Rhythmic Phase

Lifes too short to bitch and moan.

Give a sign that you've groaned.

ladio ladio ladio,

Live your life.

when you've reached the top.

Take your past and mop it up.

ladio ladio ladio,

Go Go hear the I can hear the sound.

As I travel underground.

ladio ladio ladio,

Just like a poem sometimes it rhymes.

ladio ladio ladio.

2/27/24

Can You See

Can you see me like this?

I know it's not something I wish for.

I know I cried. I never cried before.

But it's nice.

That someone out there cares.

2/27/24

Canção Da Minha Fome Por Nonas=Song Of My Hunger For Women

Quero fazer um laço com uma mulher que eu te abelha eu possa?=I want to do a loop with a woman that I want you bee I can?

Pra mim eu sonho.=For me I dream.

Porque estão livres.=Because we are free.

Pra mim eu sonho.=For me I dream.

Que está dentro do meu coração.=That 's inside my heart.

Muito muito muito,muitas muitas muitas.=Much much much,More more more.

Talvez não=Perhaps not.

Sempre assim= Always such.

Crer que quem alguém.= To believe that who is someone.

Pensa em mim.= Think of me.

Mais ae mais ae,= More ah eh,More ah eh,

Eu solitário.=I am solitary.

Me inspira ao provemos da experiência.= It inspires me ow we provide experience.

Um um dois um um dois.= One one two,one one two,

Nas moedas se passam.= The coins pass.

2/27/24

Consciência De Dos Obligaciones.=Conscience With Double duties

Y un joven que aprende dentro entiende mis=And
a youth that learns inside understands my.

Descubra.= Discovers.

Aprenda.= Learns.

Entienda.=Understands.

Y observa.= And observes.

The things in life.

Discover,Learn,Understand and Observe.

Las cosas en la vida.=Things in life.

Dos mundos que son de mi.= Two worlds that are mine.

There are two worlds that belong to me.

Hispano y Anglo parlante y a veces hablo Espangles.=Hispanic
and Anglo speaker and at times speak Spanglish.

Hay dos mundo que pertenecen a mi.= There
are two worlds that belong to me.

I am of the Hispano and Anglophone and at times I speak Espanglish.

Ahora entiendo mi deber a mi gente y a mi País.=Now
understand my duty to my people and my country.

This is the legacy that I inherited.

Now I understand the duty to my people and nation.

Este es el legado que yo herede.=This is the legacy that I inherited.

2/27/24

Single Parent

I think the game has just begun.

Father and son.

He takes him off to a football game.

Yet then he tried hockey fame.

Sonny gets sports fever.

Later on day he makes his endeavor.

What does he want to be another Joe Montana or Jack Dempsey.

The son craves sports from A-Z.

2/27/24

Presidente Não Importante=President Not Important

Todas as manhãs.= All the mornings.

Eu tenho que levar.= I have to bring.

Duas xícaras de café e pra meus pães.= Two
cups of coffee for my parents.

E pra mim um gosto e uma coisa gosto muito.=
It is a pleasure for me a thing I like a lot.

Só quero fazer muitas coisas lindas.= I only
want to do many beautiful things.

A emoção então entende a emoção.=The emotion
even though you understand the emotion.

Me levanto pra estudar e trabalhar por dentro de mim.=
I rise up to study and work for inside of me.

Sigo com um sonho mais possível.=I continue
with a dream that is more possible.

Quero ser o presidente mas não e branco , não é protestante.=I
want to be the president but not is white,not a protestant.

E porque não deixa ser.= It is because they don't let it be.

O emocao entens O emocao e uma aspiracao de
Mexicano -Americano.=The emotion you understand
is an aspiration of a Mexican-American.

Sempre vive em meu coracao.= It always lives in my heart.

Quando escuta a palavra Presidente.=When
I hear the word President.

Mas será um Tycoon de Jet Set.= But will
be a Tycoon of the Jet Set.

O homem mais poderoso e rico do mundo.=The
most powerful and richest in the world.

E foi melhor que ser Presidente dos Estados Unidos.=I was better than to be President of the United States.

Me disse meu mae no dinheiro falas mas também a boa cabeça vai bem.= My mom tells me the money speaks more and a good head goes well.

2/27/24

Solitary Heart

I have love inside my heart.

There is an unknown love very far from me.

Only I do not find her near.

I don't know her name or her race.

Could she have compassion or could she be my age?

Where does she live , what is her country?

I don't see her,but she makes me happy.

It's something I sense and am not lying.

Don't worry my solitary heart.

You'll find her like a blessed locket.

2/27/24

Quando E Que Nisto=When Is That Is?

quando é que nisto?=Whe is that is?

Meu primo chora,pobre rapazinho!= My cousin cries,poor boy!

Sim não=Yes no

Si não faça por seu bem.=If not, do it for your own good.

Talvez pelos filhos.= Perhaps for the children.

Muitas sabatina de vergonha!=Much sabbaths of shame!

Minha tia não quer esse homem.=My aunt does not want that man.

2/27/24

Bush and Quayle

Bush and Quayle leave Kuwait to Hussien.

Don't make this our own pain.

Some muslim told me why it began.

I would've gone but I'm a sole surviving son.

Bush didn't ask us for applause.

America disbelieves the war.

2/27/24

Esperance Un Momentico=Wait A Moment

La Nena quiere bailar un poquitillo.=The girl wants to dance a little.

Muevanse a mover a mover muevanse!=Move
yourselves to move to move move yourselves!

Esto el son de mi cancion.=This is the sound of my song.

Win a war without a cause.

2/7/24

Un Uomo Solo.= A Man Alone.

Quasi tutti uomini ho belle donne.= All the men have beautiful women.

Non so le ragioni.= I don't know the reasons.

Per questo desidero sapere le emozioni.= For
this I want to know the emotions.

E che la mia personalità e il mio fisico sono malevole.=It is
my personality and my physical condition are bad.

Non sapeva sì gli donne vere come uno bruto o uno belluomo.=I
did not if the ladies see how a brute or a handsome man.

Ma che il mio cuore si rotti per un incontro amb uno amore.=But
that my heart is broken from an encounter with love.

2/7/24

Jazz Improv

Yes it's true.

We could have loved.

Yes it's it's.

It could have been fun.

I was afraid.

You would reject me like all the other girls.

Who said that?"I am your friend from beginning to end.

Romance is like a dance.

I neve learned tc do it.

Sometimes I feel my heart just breaks in two.

O my love,O my love, O my love, O my love

O paramour,O paramour, O paramour,O paramour

Oui est verite.=Yes it is the truth.

Nous pouvon aimez.= We can love.

Oui est verite pouvoir.= Yes it is true we can.

2/8/24

Reunião Familiar= Family Reunion

Ahir era meu avô. =Yesterday my grandfather

Meus tios e meu primo.= My uncles and my cousin.

Sempre falavam de mim e minha irmã.= Always
they spoke of me and my sister.

Meus sons tristes que nos pra milicia.=Mine were
very sad that we were for the military.

Vou partir em 16 de dezembro e minha irmã vai em 16 de dezembro.=I
am going in december and my sister go in 16th of December.

Acordou que estava dizendo a minha tua da carta que
recebi de uns amigos.=I remember that I was saying
to my letter that I received of a few friends.

Um e dá Madrid o outro da Barcelona.= One is
from Madrid or another from Barcelona.

Acho que meus amigos na repostas.=I think
that my friends the answers.

3/7/24

Estudo Na Manhã Estudio En La Ma~nana Study In The Morning

Trabalho na meia noite Trabajo en la madrugada I work in the midnight.

7 dias da semana 7 dias en la semana 7 seven days out of the week.

Parara parara pra pra

Parara parara pra pra

Pra e nao se quando descanso Y no se cuando
descanso And I don't know when I'm resting.

Não sei quando eu vou Y no se cuando voy
I don't know when I'm going to.

Você eris na mulher eu nao sou homem Tu eres la mujer Yo
no soy su hombre You are the women I am not the man.

Diz-me um pouco pra entems Di me un pouco
entiendes . Tell me a little so understand.

Eu sinto a cantiga Siento el canto I can feel the blues.

Sinto o fado e velho Siento el cante jondo y es
viejo. I can feel the blues and it is old.

Eu ver nao pode tenher Yo mire no puedo tener I see I don't have.

3/8/24

Quando Faco De Escrever Nas Palavras=When
I Type The Written Words.

Se me vai é muito difícil pra mim.= It is very difficult for me.

De expressar que está O meu coração dá repente.=Of
expressing that it is my heart of repeatedly.

Eu sinto que a inteligência entra por mim.=I feel
that the intelligence enters by me.

Em minha cabeça e também no meu corpo.=
In my head and also my body.

Sou feliz e estou contente.=I am happy and am also content.

Que agora nas palavras é muito fácil.= Now
that the words are very easy.

3/8/24

Eu Quero Um Vinho Doce.= I want a sweet wine.

um vinho pra acompanhar o tempo.= A wine to accompany the time.

Que é isso meu desejo hoje sem palavras.= What
is that my desire today without words.

Que dizer ontem quando na primeira vez.= What
to say yesterday when it was the first time.

Que pode provar no vinho.= That I could taste the wine.

Um vinho doce que eu bebo.=A wine sweet that I can drink.

3/8/24

Aprender Català= Learn Catalan

Meu amic està hi Barcelona.= My friend is in Barcelona.

On que parla català.= Here that Catalan is spoken.

Una llengua que se parla six million de personnes.=
A language spoken by six million persons.

El se alegre perquè jo vull parlar hi català.=He is
glad because I want to speak in Catalan.

Nunca vi sua vida, esperei que una persona quer aprender.=Never
seen in his life,wait until a person wants to learn.

El me escrit hi lletra que seu llengua es popular per les olympiades.=
He writes in a letter that his language is popular for the olympics.

Es com un astre vola per el ar.= ts like a
celestial body flying through the air.

Record quan jo l'he dit Catalunya tenen seu renaixença.=I
remember when I told them Catalonia has their rebirth.

Per aquesta raó jo és molt goig.=For this reason I am very joyous.

3/8/24

Aprender Català= Learn Catalan

Pega el pez.= Hit the fish.

Ah Ah

Pega el solar plexis.= Hit the solar plexus.

Ah Ah

El bozal componen su alma= The muzzle composes his soul.

3/8/24

Barri Difficile Per Me.= Neighborhood Is Hard For Me.

Cadascú tenen seu LLibertats .= Each one has their liberties.

Meu amic voler anar bras di bras.= My friend wants to walk arm in arm.

Meus amics anant per la carrera cuales vols.= My
friends walk for the street how many want.

Queixos cuales vols= They which want.

Queixos si vaig la seu casa es per la nit o matí.=They do
come to their home it is by the night or morning.

Per mi et dificil quan tornaré com meu pai.= It
is difficult when I return like my priest.

Per il barri per ara.= For the neighborhood for now.

Per il barri per ara.=For the neighborhood for now.

340

3/8/24

Cada Fin De Semana=Each Weekend

Yo consigo boletos complementarios como Juana y varios.= I get complimentary tickets like Jane and others.

En algo en particular.= In something in particular.

Quieren ver un espectacular?= Do you want to see a spectacle.

Que es una comedia o un musical o una tragedia.= Which is like a comedy or a musical or a tragedy.

Deu Deu Deudo.=Debt

Conexiones,emociones,inspiraciones son canciones.=Connections,emotions,inspirations are songs.

Truene,truene,truene,truene.=Shine,Shine,Shine,Shine.

todo entretenimiento para mis familiares, entretenimientos para mis amistades.=All entertainment for my family and friends.

Siempre quiero bailar, siempre quiero cantar, siempre quiero tocar y actuar.=Always I want to dance,always I want to sing,always I want to play and act.

Cada fin de semana deu deu deudo.= Each weekend deu deu debt.

Agora Eu Vou Pra Milícia.= I Go To The Military.

Minha irmã vai pra área forca.= My sister goes to the Airforce.

Eu digo minha phuri dai.=I say to my grandmother.

Não vou ficar por um tempo, não te vejo.= I will not
be here for some time I will not see you.

Quem ninguém sabe que fazer.= Who one knows what to do.

Vou servir cinco anos de milícia como um mentalista.=
I will serve 5 years of military like a mentalist.

Hoje não trabalho e estudo.= Today I don't work and study.

Quando eu serei ator.= When will I be an actor?

Quando eu me caso.= When I will be married.

Hoje à noite vou alugar minha antiga casa um duplex apartamentos.=
Tonight I will rent my ancient house and duplex apartments.

Quando eu baile minha irmã vai pra aéreo força isto é
que e dizer a meu tio.= When I dance my sister is going
to the air force this is what I say to my uncle.

Eu vejo a lua.= I see the moon.

Minha prima falou com meus p~aes e irmã.= My
cousin speaks to my parents and sister.

Brilhar meus p~aes ver na televisão.=To brighten my parents see the tv.

Minha irmã fala com meus p~aes outra irmã vai dormir.=My
sister speaks with my parents and the other sister goes to bed.

Acho de meu nome que e lua também.=I think
of my name which is moon too.

Esta noite minha prima chamou a nossa casa.=
This night my cousin called to our house.

Minha mãe chamou a Los Angeles pra conversar com meu tio,primo e outra prima e tia.= My mom called to los Angeles to talk to my uncle,cousin and my other cousin and aunt.

Tambem eu falei com eles e menos minha tia.= I also spoke with them and at the least with my aunt.

Que eu vou na milícia pra fazer um cabo E-3. = That I go to the military to become a Private First Class E-3.

3/9/24

Pauvre Estats Units n'est pas ou est mon pays d'or.=Poor
United States it is not my country of gold.

Jamais ne serait- il payé de l'argent.= It will no
longer be a country of Silver money.

Aujourd'hui, aux Etats Unis il sont payés très pauvre.=
Today the United States is country very poor.

Les enfants meurent de faim.= The babes die of hunger.

Les gens manquent de travail.= The people lack work.

Le studente n'est pas de monnaie.= The students don't have the purse.

Il président promesse promesse con mot mais non fait
L'actions.=The president promises promises but does no action.

Seulement nous avons de la misère que donnez le recession.=
Only we have the misery that the recession gives.

Mon coeur de dolores pour mois futur.= My
heart of the pains for my future.

J'ai desole = I am sorry.

3/9/24

El Jorn= The Day

El Jorn que meu pare el cabo la casita.=The day
that my father the cape the little house.

El no colorear la.= He will not color it.

El meu déu que et per seu neta qui vine hi futur.=He told me that
and it was for his granddaughter who was coming in the future.

3/9/24

Oggi parlato con una bella donna.= Today I
have spoken with a beautiful woman.

Ella di Bologna.= She is from Bologna.

Occhiali Azzurri con il capello biondo.= Blue eyes with blond hair.

Ella è andata con suo marito e amici.= She is
going with her husband and friends.

Vada in treno a Tijuana,Mesico'= She is on a
train bound for Tijuana,Mexico.

Io gli ho detto spero la sia stata buona per lei. suo marito e amici.=
I told her I await the stay is good with your husband and friends.

Richiami al suo marito per sentarsi.=We ask
that your husband to sit down.

Ma io vedo i capelli e gli occhiali di suo marito qui o no castagno
e bello come sua moglie.=But I see the hair and eyes of your
husband which are not chestnut beautiful like your wife.

Le due sono una belle maritare io desidero a parlare con le due.=You
two are the beautiful marriage to speak with the two of you.

Raccordo qui io detto Ciao,A Dio.= I remember
that I said farewell,goodbye.

Viaggio al cuore e belle signorini.=Trip to the heart and beautiful men.

Che lei saprai vado a la sua.= That you know I'm coming to yours.

3/9/24

Prado meu aquesta o céu.= The meadow is mine, that was the sky.

Prado meu eu tenho que seguir no camalhão.= On
my meadow I have to follow no camouflage.

Não pode virar atrás sempre avante.=I cant turn back always in front.

Prado Meu Na batalha começa meu coração.=My
meadow the battle starts my heart.

Impeça a luta em batalha.=He starts to fight in the battle.

Pra o milicia nao facil fazer minho trabalho.=For
the military it is not easy to do my job.

Isto é para mim uma casa dificultosa.=It is for me a hard house.

Prado meu a que está o céu.= My meadow of which is the sky.

346

3/10/24

Escoltar Radio = They Hear The Radio

Quan escolto lles cants de la radio.=When I hear the song on the radio.

Jo penso hi todas las inspiració per amor e molts anys.=I
think of all the inspirations for a love and many years.

De experiencia totas les melodies que foi fet per les altres.=Of
experience of all the melodies that were done to others.

La poble que vols escoltar.= The village that I want to hear.

Las cancions que vaig fora de cor so le flors cue brotan ara.=The
songs that go outside out of the only the flowers that blossom now.

3/10/24

Er Mestizhe Ibero-Americano= The Mixture Ibero-American

Somo lo mima la gente.= We are the same people.

Tu no sabe la hitoria de tu abolengo.= You don't
know the history of your heritage.

En tu vena eta sangre Cale,Arabe,Moruna, Judía
y un poco Celtibera.= In your veins is the blood of
Gypsies, Arabs,Berbers,Jews and Celticiberian.

No hay gente ma rica en herencia.=There is people
with much richness in inheritance.

Por tu lao de lo indigena te viene lo mejor del pasao.=From
your indigenous you come from the best of the past.

3/10/24

Sol Due Parole= Only Two Words

Sol due per me=Only two for me.

O Ancora,O Ancora= Oh still , oh still.

Tu saprai,il giovane non ha la sua signora.=You know,the youngman does not have his miss.

Questo e a mia storia e vero.= This is my story it is true.

Ti desidero o ancora o ancora.= I want oh still,oh still.

Caro occhiali dime dove stai o ancora o ancora.= Dear eyes tell me where is she oh still,oh still.

Dove fu bella signorina fiore di vita.=Where were you beautiful damsel flower of life.

Sol due parole sol due parole per me o ancora, o ancora.=Only two words only two words for me oh still,oh still.

3/10/24

Lavori Propi= One's Own work.

El cel blau es poc blanc et roser.= The sky blue is less white and pink.

Ara est nit mes que mai.= Now is night more than never.

Jo vist le car estacio per meu casa.= I see my car parked at my house.

Tot el poble vaig a teatro per viure l'actuació de seu producció.=All the town is going to the theater to see the acts of its production.

Mes jo estudi la llengua Catala.= But I study the Catalan language.

Cadascú ten seu propi lavori.=Each one of us has their own work.

3/10/24

Ma vie Sans Les Beau choses.=My Life Without The Good Things

Avez Vous, Avec Vous de votre maison?.=Do
you have,do you have your home?

Quez Vous, Avezvous d'argent?= Do you have your money?

Avez vous,Avez vous de belle femme?.=Have
you, Have you of the beautiful.

Avez vous,avez vous de voiture de bonne
chance?=Do you have a car of good luck?

Mon Ami c'est la vie.=My friend, that's life.

Mon ami c'est la vie.=My friend, that's life.

Jen ou vous pas porquoi.= J'en why are you not here.

Ma vie coeure.= My life's heart.

Tu connais ma vie sans les beau choses.= You
know my life without the beautiful things.

Je suis desole.= I'm sorry.

Je sens comment le désert.=I feel like the desert.

Pourquoi Je n'ai pas fait les bonnes choses?=Why
I don't do the good things?

3/10/24

Give

Give me some spice To break the ice.

The seasons fly away.

I spend it studying languages.

I weight lift until I'm exhausted.

I train till,breathless.

I save so I'm no longer penniless.

Sius Plau=Please

El cel blau.= The blue sky.

Perdoni sius plau.=Sorry please.

Jo vull una noia bell.= I want a beautiful girl.

Molt lluny non puny.= Much far not fist.

3/18/24

Molts Anys=Many Years

Siusplau meu Déu ajuda me perque son sóc feliç.=Please
my GOD help me because I'm not happy.

Ara jo vull ser llibert fer molts cosas per la pau..=I
want to be free to do many things for peace.

Volto a guerra si non ha la pau per me i meva família.= I
return to war if there is no peace for me or my family.

Cada any se perdeu hi un espaciu que non tingui fin.=
Each year loses a space that doesn't have an end.

Sempre non tenc amics de veritats,=I don't always have true friends.

Ningú sap que jo sóc enojat molts scu un soldat.=Noone knows
that I am extremely annoyed because I am a soldier.

La guerre sigui per molts anys jo vull justica non tinc pau hi meu
ment la lluita dur molt mal.=The war follows for many years. I want
justice I don't have peace in my mind the fight is hard very bad.

Quan es que podeu tenc la pau hi meva vida.=
When I can I will have peace in my life.

Qui és meu amic o amiga de veritat.= Who is my friend truly.

Sempre lo mesmo que tinc plorar per manque la
Justica.=I always have to cry for lack of Justice.

Ara non vaig a la sinagoga que vulls pau i justica.= Now I
don't go to the synagogue that wants peace and justice.

Dintre meu cor sempre andate a la guerra.= Inside
my heart is always wondering about the war.

El cami es dur i plen de adversitat.= The
road is hard and full of adversity.

Jorn i nit no podeu estat calme.= Day and night I can't be calm.

Quan jo vencit a meu inimics jo fet justica hi mi vida.=When
I vanquish my enemies we will do justice in my life.

3/18/24

Os Dias= The Days

Os dias passam pra mim no hospital ninguém sabe
que aconteceu com mim.=The days past for me in the
hospital no one knows what happened to me.

As horas passam também dias do luz cheios de raios do sol.=The
hours pass also the days of light are full of the sun rays.

Às vezes é noite de chuva fria.= At times night of cold rain.

Tenho muita saudade dos tempos passados quando terei Família.=
I have a lot of longing for times past when I had a family.

Agora nao possivel pra mim estar com eles.=
Now it's not possible to be with them.

Eu sou um desterrado dos meus sobrinhos.=I
am buried alive by my nephews.

Neles não me querem pra nada Eu sou estrangeiro a
minha gente por meus inimigos.=They don't love me for
nothing. I am a stranger to my people by my enemies.

Todo pra mim se volta em uma tomba.= It turns into a tomb.

Eu sou enterrado em vida por minha familha , os
compatriotas e ex amizades tornam-se adversários.

Só Deus vai fazer justiça com tudo mundo.= Only
GOD can make justice with the whole world.

Porque tenho que fazer vingança contra meus inimigos.=Because
I had to take revenge against my enemies.

Quando isso passar vou estar feliz para o fim da minha
vida.=When that happens I will be happy to the end of my life.

03/19/24

Cu Un Giorno=It's One Day

Che un giorno io sono stato in hospedale.=It's
one day I have been in the hospital.

Come fato per la salute, bene o male.=How
is it done for my health or disease.

C Io sono molto pieno di paura al dente.=I
am filled with fear of the tooth.

Riconosciuto di mente che fai ancora di repente.= I
don't recognize the mind of what I do suddenly.

Uno sai lui signore angelo e pazzo come Io.= One
knows you mister angel and crazy like me.

Stanco e manco di forza per Lutare moltissimo.=
Tired and lacking strength to fight a lot.

Signore Angelo e pazzo come io.=Mister angel is crazy like me.

Ci sono pieno di coraggio in la guerra.= I am full of courage in the war.

Tutti i frontalieri chi portano l'arma.= All fronts that carry arms.

Quando io andiamo in fretta succede che sono più
lento.=When I go in a hurry it occurs very slowly.

03/23/24

¿Qué pasa?= What 's Happening?

Que me pasa con la raza dicen el gigante dormido?=What
is happening with the race says the sleeping giant?

Asi es que Dios lo ha querido!=That is how God has wanted it!

Tienes que ser valiente y no serás vencido!=You must
be valiant and you shall not be defeated!

Lo que pasa conmigo es el temor que siente mi ombligo.=What
is happening to me is the terror that my belly button feels.

?Que es mi destino no soy mezquino?=What
is my destiny I am not meaning?

Mexicanos y chicanos levántense si se puede!= Mexicans
and MexicanAmericans rise, yes you can!

No te quedes aún lo mereces.=Don't remain
even though you deserve it.

Mi raza es crema y nata de la Corona Española.=My people
are the cream of the crop for the crown of Spain.

3/23/24

El Tyempo=The Time

Munchos lokos atavandos.=Many crazies to the ceiling.

Sufrieron la shoah komo reskapados.=They
suffered the holocaust like shaved heads.

Todos sus kaveyos hueron arapados.=
All their hairs were shaved.

Eyos se toparon en sinagogas vaziyas.=They
found themselves in empty schuls.

La shoah era tyempo pretos.= The holocaust was dark times.

Los Almanes no mos tuvyeron respeto a mozotros los
sefardim.=The Germans did not have respect for us Spanish Jews.

Dunke si avia un nazi piadozo perkilozo por el o eya si turvyera
kompasyon de mozotroz.= If there was a compasionate nazi
it was dangerous if he or she had compassion on us

Stava hazino enjunto mis chaverim de maale de Yavan.Mos
pudimos entender ke ez ser haragan=I was sick with my friends of
the greek neighborhood.we could understand what was lazy.

Muestras famiyas hueron kremadas i non son ulvidadas.=
Our families were cremated and not forgotten.

El chachambashi de Grezya fue matado er el krematorium i los
de Rodos,Larisa,Corfu i Makedonya ainda menos los de sefardim
de Bulgaria i Turkia no hue la muerte para eyos.=The grand
Rabbi of Greece was killed in the crematorium and those of
Rhodes,Larisa,Corfu and Macedonia even though the Spanish
Jews of Bulgaria and Turkey did not get death for them.

Los sefardis ke stavan en otras partes del mundo tambyen
salvados por Hashem el Dio pyadozo,ke mos kyeri komo
su djente eskojida.= The Spanish Jews that were in other
parts of the world were also saved by The name the
most Merciful,that he loved his chosen people.

Sobrevivimos el couchemal de los frankos ma esto fue una vedradera,miserya.Agora los ke no mos fazyeron eskperimentos pudimos tener fijos i famiya.=We survived the nightmare of the franks but this was a true misery now those who did not get experimented were able to have children and family.

Days

The days go by the sun,it goes down.Before it hits the ground.The rays of the sun are strong for the day is long. Time in a flutter makes for one's bread and butter. I feel the day,like it stuttersKnow the seconds,minutes,hours are passing in a row. it's watching a doe.How must I pass the hard times of a day with rhyme.Being a poet I am fine. The day with sunlight will shine.Am I mortal or divine of days gone.I seems the day is done. When will the glory and magic return. So I'm ecstatic for a cartoon. I want to feel the rays of the sun.

I want to go to the beach to have fun.

03/23/24

Drole=Crazy

Je ne suis drôle mais normal.=I am not crazy but normal.

La famille pense que j'ai perdu la sanite.=My
family thinks I have lost my sanity.

Pour moi je heine le mode de réflection de mon amitié=For
me I hate the type of reflection of my friendship.

Je ne sais pas quelle est la raison de maladie.=I
don't know the reason of the sickness.

Elles ne font pas le pitie pour ma situation.=She does not pity me.

La vent est gris n'est pas du soleil.=The cloud is gray, it is not the sun.

Voudriez que la chose changer.=Would you
like for me to change a thing.

tout le monde connaît mon histoire.=The
whole world knows my history.

Me manque la savoire faire.= I lack the know how.

Comment est possible la situation non améliorée?.=
Will it possible for my situation to not get better?

Désire beaucoup d'argent pour payer les comptes.=
I desire a lot of money to pay my bills.

Seul Dieu me répondra pour ma vie.=Only God will respond for my life.

03/23/24

Mabuhay=Long live

Mabuhay kaibigan Ekstranhero=Long live my foreign friends.

Magandang Umaga Pilipinas.=Good Morning Philippines.

Araw-araw pwede magluto Pagkain Pilipino.=Day
to Day we can cook Filipino food.

Araw mabuti Magsulat ng kanta-kanta.= Today is good to write songs.

May guapa pinay Ginang Puti.=Very good looking Mrs.White.

Gusto Ko kumain Turon,Halo-halo,Taho at Buho Ice cream.=
I like eating Turon,Halo-halo, Taho and Buho Ice cream.

Mahal kita Ginang Puti,Magkita Kita.= I love
you Mrs.White,you are my dear.

Teka pero ng kalahating oras nang hapon.=Wait
but in half hour of the afternoon.

Sige sa gabi.=Ok this next night.

Ako pag-ibig mo para sa Ginang Mabuhay por syempre.=I
have love for Mrs.White long live for always for sure.

Maraming salamat po pagbisita.= Thank very much for the visit.

Paalam na sinyora Puti a las 10 na.=Goodbye Mrs.White at 10pm.

03/24/24

Quero Ser Ciebe=I Want To Be Free

Eu deseixo a Ciebedade porque te~no saudade.=I desire freedom because I have longing.

Ni moi o menos fazemos un novo País.=Not more or less make us a new country.

Que crer en libertade que moitos rezpiren seu ar livre.=Who believes in freedom that many want to breathe their free air.

Naixemos por un dia e noite para mi e un escoite.=We're born for one day and night for me and one hidden.

Vivemos todos Xuntos sempre en unidade Galicia,Asturies,,Castillaleon,Cantabria,Irlanda,Escoca ,Breto~na,Gales,Cornualles,Isla do Home.=We live together in always in unity Galicia,Asturias,Castilla leon,Cantabria,Ireland,Scotland,Brittany,Wales,Isle of Man.

Quen para Que seamos uns so Deus no proteixe como pescar o peixe.=Who are that we are one only God protects us like fishing a fish.

Voltaches comigo cami~nando xuntos al novo pais e punto.= If you don't walk with us together to the new country and point.

Meu Corazon chora por sua familia Celta sempre atoparos.=My heart cries for its Celtic family always it finds us.

Dainda moi canso da guerra Queremos moita paz.=Even though I am tired of war we want much peace.

Incheme da groria da nosa istoria.=Fill me with the glory of our history.

03/24/24

Mujerika=Little Woman

Mujerika eresh guapina sefardita de Asturies.=Little woman you are a beauty Sephardic of Asturias.

Komeros fabada i djudiyas vedres kon peixe=We will eat navy beans and green beans with fish.

Un pokitiko de yayin kon lejem de chabat.=A little **bit of wine and bread for the sabbath.**

Ansi dizi mi mujer ma mujerika la yamo un diya.= So goes my wife little lady I call you one day.

3/24/24

Días De Sol= Sunny Days

Días de sol como un caracol que tiene múltiples niveles de Sotol.=Days of like a snail of multiple levels of axolotl spirit.

Me gusta andar en la playa que bueno que no estoy en la halla.=I like being at the beach it's a good thing I'm not at the Hague.

Agradezco a Dios por darme mi voz, no quiero ser atroz.=I thank God for giving me my voice I don't want to be cruel.

La hechura de una mujer vestida con un parasol.= The making of a woman dressed in a parasol.

Me hace un plato de frijol.= Makes me a plate of beans.

Estoy atrayendo me curiosidades.= I am attracting me curiosities.

Estar en el sol o bajo chaparrales.=To be in the sun or below the bushes.

Haci es en todas las comunidades ir al colegio de las fraternidades=That is how it is in all the communities we go to the college of the fraternities.

Día de sol me aguanto vivo la vida no la espanto.=Day of the sun I can bear. I live life not the scare.

Cuando tengo a mi novia el amor que es bueno vivo mejor.=When I have my girlfriend the love I have shows how good I live better.

Quiero ser el único hombre para ti una vez.=I want to be the only man for you once.

Tu cariño de mi a ti talvez.=Your caresses of me to you perhaps.

El Revés de mi se acaba el estrés.= The reverse of me finishes the stress

04/17/24

Studying In The Morning= Estudio en la mañana

Trabajo en la madrugada.=I work the nightshift.

Siete días a la semana.= Seven days out of the week.

Parara, Parara

Y no se cuando voy a descansar= And I don't know when going to rest.

Tu eres la mujer = You are the woman.

Y no soy el hombre =And I'm not the man.

Dime un poco para entender.=Tell me a little so I can understand.

Siento el canto y es muy viejo.= I can feel the blues that is old news.

Yo miro no Yo puedo.=I see I can't.

Yo deseo recogerla.=I wish I could grab it.

04/17/24

Desilucion Teatre= Theatrical Disillusion

He tratado de escalar poco a poquito un poco más.=I
have tried to go up a little bit more or less.

En vez de ir atrás quiero ir en frente.=Instead
of going back I want to go front.

Aunque no he conseguido .= Even though I have gotten it.

Anhelo estar por la pantalla vestido de gala.= There I
long to be in the scene dressed for the occasion.

04/17/24

Cristina=Christine

Hay una chica que no me deja solo!=There is a
young girl that doesn't leave me alone!

Es una colega se entrega.=She is a colleague that gives herself.

No más seremos amistad.= We will not be friends anymore.

Tienes que aceptar la realidad.= You have to accept the reality.

Los dos somos dos culturas, dos idiomas y dos religiones.=
We are of two cultures,two languages and two religions.

Dos personas distintas así se pintan.= Two
distinct persons that is how it's painted.

Hay horas en cual no deseo conversar o convivir.= There are
hours in which there is no desire to converse or share bread.

04/17/24

Yo Fui= I Was

Yo fui a una fiesta como un caballero a la reconquista.=
I went to a party like a gentleman to the crusade.

Y te mire como la doncella timida= And I
saw how timide the maiden was.

Un vero amor verdadero.= A true love truly.

Yo te quiero un amor verdadero=I want you a true love.

Somos una juventud inocente llena de virtud.=We
are innocent youth full of virtue.

Era yo te quiero primera vista=I was that I love you from first view.

Un amor verdadero yo te quiero!=A true love I want!

Después bailamos en la pista Yo te quiero.= Later
we dance on the dance floor I want to.

Yo te quiero no esperaba nada.= I want you, I did not expect you.

Yo vine con mi primo.= I came with my cousin.

No sabia pero alli estabas.=I didn't know you were there.

Ahora te estimo Yo te quiero Un amor verdadero.=
Now I esteem I love you a true love.

¡Lastima que vivo muy lejos de ti!=What a pity to live far from you!

Solo ruego que me beses a mi.= Only I beg you that you kiss me.

Es una emoción que siento aquí.=Its an emotion that I feel here.

Por dentro mi corazón Yo te quiero.= For deep in my heart I want you.

Yo te quiero amor verdadero yo te quiero.=
I love you my true love I love you.

04/17/24

Sometimes

Sometimes I need you and you're not near

YOu are something so to my heart.

I love you with all my soul .

You fill me with tranquility.

This is what you can be for me.

UUH UUH UUh UUh

la ,la lara la la lara

aah aah aah

You are the girl that can be taken for a cruise in La Jolla.

Also I'll take them to the beach for a picnic.

I want to buy all the things in the Shopping Malls.

So that I wine and dine you in an expensive restaurant.

Give you a fur coat with a diamond bracelet.

Instill your tenderness and give me momentary bliss.

Lala la ra la lalara

aah aah aaah

Show me how to live.

Make me feel like a man.

Emotionally and physically only you.

11/28/24

Nadal=Christmas

Bon nadal et any nou.=Merry Christmas and Happy New Year.

Agora vinguis a la esglesias.= Now you come to the churches.

El pare amb mare vaig les fills et fillas.= The father
with mother comes with sons and daughters.

Per viure un xocolat cald.=For drinking a hot chocolate.

Ningu sapiga que manjar tomaquet.= No One
knew what it was to eat tomatoes.

El jorn aneu a la sagrada per visitar non vull anar per me.=The
day comes to be sacred to visit. I don't want to walk with me.

La nit de nit bona es felic.=The night of good night is happy.

Totalment no sentit de alegria gran meu cor.=Totally
not a sense of happiness a great my heart.

11/28/24

Maligaya Pasko=Merry Christmas

Maligaya Pasko kumusta kaibigan.=Merry
Christmas how are you friend.

Sige na dito para sa regalos sa loob ang pader.=Go
here next for the gifts inside the wall.

Komain pagkain Pilipino Turon,Halohalo,champorado,arroz caldo.
=Eat Filipino food Turon,Halo Halo,Champorado,Arros Kaldo.

Paalam kaibigans.=Good bye friends.

Mabuhay at Maligaya Pasko noche buena ang Paskua.=Long
life and Merry Christmas this Christmas Eve and Merry.

11/28/24

Dia De Ação De Graça = Thanksgiving Day

Ninguém sabe o que é a Turquia com Gustavo.=
No one knows turkey Gustav.

Primeira volta sem mãe e tia.= First time without mom and aunty.

Tudo isso foi que sentia.=Everything that I felt.

Pra mim o inhame doce para você.= For me the sweet yams for you.

A vida tem surpresas porque tudo está na mesa.= Life
has surprises because everything is on the table.

Só eu quero vinho pra beber isso esclarecer.=I
want to drink wine to clarify.

Por mim acho assim.=For me I think like this.

11/28/24

Second Time

Second time where is my rhyme.

Thanksgiving day I climbed away.

Toucher, it's time to play.

Turkey,mash,cranberry sauce, it is stuffing not moss.

I'm not at home with mom,tia trine and Jerome.

Take things lightly and finish the food sprightly.

11/28/24

Veces Que?=What times?

A veces son reveses porque mi familia me hiere.=At
times its reverses why does my family hurt me.

Como a mi no me quire.=Like me they don't love me.

Ni la hoja del brazo baja al ocaso.=Nor the
leaf of the branch lowers to sunset.

Quien lo dice así porque yo perdí=who said
it was like that because I lost.

No los puedo ver a mi hermanita, sus hijos y ~nietos.=.I can't
see them my sister ,her children and grandchildren.

Para mi es un vacío uno con desafio.=For
me its a void that is a challenge.

Yo tengo que tener mi propia familia porque me han desterrado.=I
must have my own family because they have buried me alive.

De pelear estoy cansado.=Of fighting I am tired.

Para que viviré es mucho pedir.- To live it 's too much to ask.

cuando se vaya mi madre igual que mi padre.=When
my mom goes same as my father.

Solo a Dios tendre.= Only GOD I will have.

11/28/24

Bichiami Andro=I am Called Andro.

Bichiami Andro no Alessandro.=Im called Andrò not Alessandro.

Perché non mi piace?=Why will it not please me?

Tutti i giorni senza spumoni dopo.=All the days without spumoni later.

Parlo molto un po 'di troppo.=I speak a lot.

Abbiamo la chiesa di San Guido.=We have the church of San Guido.

Mangiamo una pizza chiara scura.=We eat a dark light pizza.

Io prego a Dio Benedetti a me a mia famigghia.=I
pray to GOD to bless me and my family.

Quando venerdì sapevo la mia bucca mangiare il pesce che non
cresce.=When friday I know my mouth eats the fish that doesnot grow.

Ciao a tutti mangia frutti.=Farewell to all that consume fruit.

03/27/25

I Need You

I need and you are not near,

You are something so near to my heart.

I love you with all my soul.

You fill me with tranquility.

This is what you can be for me

OOH OOH UUh OOH

LA LA LARA LA LA LARA

You are the girl that can be taken for a cruise in La Jolla.

Also I'll take you to the beach of Coronado for a picnic.

I want to buy all the things in the Shopping Malls.

So that you wine and dine you in expensive restaurant.

Give you fur coat with a diamond bracelet.

Instill your tenderness give me momentary bliss.UUH UUH UUH UUH

LA LALARA LALA LARA

Show me how to live.

Make me feel like a man.

Emotionally and physically.

Only you can.

Fiesta =Party

Yo fui a una fiesta= I went to a feast.

Como un caballero a la reconquista=Like a knight in the reconquest.

Y te mire como la doncella timida=I saw you like a timid damsel.

Yo te quiero.= I love you.

Un amor verdadero.=A True love.

Yo te quiero

Somos la juventud inocentes y llenos de virtud=We
are innocent youth and full of virtue.

Yo te quiero

Un amor verdadero

Yo te quiero.